The History of Bemrose School, Derby

A Celebration in Words and Pictures of the First 75 years (1930 – 2005)

Written and Compiled by

Leanne Baker, Marilyn Thompson and Donald T Sarfas

With

Personal Contributions from Old Bemrosians

A commissioned publication on behalf of BFPA

23 Park Road, Ilkeston, Derbys DE7 5DA
Tel: 0115 932 0643 www.moorleys.co.uk

ISBN 978 0 86071 620 4

British Library Cataloguing in Publication Data.
A catalogue record for this book is available
from the British Library.

Printed from data supplied electronically

MOORLEYS
Print & Publishing

23 Park Road, Ilkeston, Derbys DE7 5DA
Tel: 0115 932 0643 www.moorleys.co.uk

This book is dedicated to the memory of

Stanley William Tacey
born 4th January 1920, died 24th December 2007

He won a scholarship from Kedleston Road
Primary School to Bemrose School and was in the
first intake in September 1930.
He was a hard working scholar who used his
education to the full, a real friend to all who knew
him.

ACKNOWLEDGEMENTS

As the only non-Bemrosian, Marilyn Thompson has been instrumental in the production of this account of the first 75 years of the School. It is with a real sense of gratitude that I acknowledge a very considerable personal effort over several years. Thank you, Marilyn, on behalf of many generations of Bemrosians. This is probably one of the last Parkfield Cedars/Bemrose joint efforts of various "kinds" to have been successful!

Others who have contributed to whole or part chapters are as follows:

Leanne Baker	Tom Kemple	Arthur Titterton
Richard Feist	Robert Leighton	Brian Waters
Peter Good	Dennis Monk	Ken Walters
Alan Gifford	Hugh Price	Jo Ward
Peter Grattidge	Anton Rippon	

I thank them all for their help. As the editor of their contributions I can only apologise if I have given any concern in pressing the "delete" key which is the 2008 equivalent of the 1930 red pencil! Such is progress.

Donald T. Sarfas

1930 plaque at the School entrance steps
Photo courtesy Andy Savage www.derbyphotos.co.uk

CONTENTS

Copyright Holders of photographs
Co-operation in the use of these photographs
is greatly appreciated.

DERBY EVENING TELEGRAPH
Pages 8, 61, 65, 72, 79, 95, 111 and 143.

DERBYSHIRE ADVERTISER
Pages 22, 23, 25 and 27.

DERBY EXPRESS
Page 39.

ANDY SAVAGE   www.derbyphotos.co.uk

Pages 4, 16, 19, 23, 128, 138, 150, 153, 154, 161 and 162.

W. W. WINTERS
Page 23.

PICTURE THE PAST
Page 137.

INTRODUCTION

By Marilyn D Thompson

It seems as though Bemrose School has always played a part in my life. As a child, I was brought up on St Albans Road, and four times daily I would pass the hallowed grounds of Bemrose School on my way to College Primary School.

In my teenage years, as a pupil of Parkfield Cedars, I would admire the Bemrose boys who ran past our house, taking part in the Cross Country runs.

My father, Thomas Hoult, was Deputy Headmaster of Rykneld School and later joined the staff at Bemrose when the two schools combined. He spent most of his teaching time in the Albany Road annexe which was known to the staff as 'Stalag'. I helped in Rykneld School library in the early 80's, but it was not until 1990 that I joined the Bemrose staff, having spent my earlier career as school library adviser to Derbyshire County.

I enjoyed my 14 years at the school, before health problems led to early retirement.

During my time as school librarian I conserved and valued the archives and history of the school, and many ex pupils would visit to library to view the files of magazines, programmes and photos. It was on one such visit that I was introduced to Donald Sarfas.

The rest – as they say – is history.

By Leanne Baker

Although I left school with no clear idea of what work I should do, I soon found that the education I had received had equipped me to do many things. One of these was to help my employer (Derek Latham, Architect) write and publish a book. My main task was to select and insert photographs into the text.

In this book not only have I added the many photographs, but as one of the first girls to attend the school, contributed to the text.

By Donald T Sarfas

Little did I realise when I walked out of Bemrose School in December 1936 that 72 years later I would write an introduction to the History of the School.

Those of us who were fortunate enough to be among the first intake in September 1930 did not give a moment's thought to the idea that we were entering upon an exceptional educational adventure. It was only when we were making our way in the world after the 1939-45 war, that we appreciated our good fortune in attending such a splendid school. The Bygones pages of the Derby Evening Telegraph have awakened fond memories from many Old Boys. It is from these reminiscences that the idea of a History of Bemrose School has become a reality.

Whilst ever it stands, the building is a fitting memorial to Alderman H. H. Bemrose, who was Chairman of the Education Committee in the 1920s. When it opened, the building was at the edge of town. The town has become a city and a large proportion of the population now resides in the areas outside the ring road. New schools have been built in these areas, with the result that Bemrose School is now an "inner city" school. The building has additions, and the pupils of today are from many different cultures. In a recent intake, the pupils had over 30 different mother tongues. Today the school is a microcosm of the world: colour, ethnic origin, language, and innate abilities.

This volume, with some information about its forerunner the Derby Municipal Secondary School in Abbey Street, is an account of secondary education since this became a local authority concern after the Education Act of 1902. It covers 75 years of changes.

Donald and Marilyn
Photo courtesy Derby Evening Telegraph

The Bygones pages were the initiators, Councillor David Black was overwhelmed by the response and Marilyn Thompson, the School Librarian, told me on my first visit that she was looking for someone to organise it, I said that if I ever came back to Derby I might have a go. My wife and I were very happily retired in Pembrokeshire and, while it was a possibility, I did not foresee it happening so soon. I came back to Derbyshire in 1999.

After some research I found Geoff Horton who was the organiser of the Old Bemrosian Grammarian Association's (OBGA) annual Golf Day and Dinner. With the aid of my lifelong and sadly late friend Stan Tacey, my form captain from 1930, we arranged a Grammarian Association dinner in November 2002. It was there that, encouraged by Richard Feist the Head Teacher, I floated the idea of a history and this was met with much enthusiasm. The Governing Board approved.

Marilyn Thompson, ex Parkfield Cedars, had just retired and willingly took up the task of gathering, selecting, and arranging the material as the first step to publication. I can reasonably claim to have launched the "History" but the hard work has been done with enthusiasm and skill by Marilyn. I much appreciate the special contribution of those who, with a little persuasion from Marilyn, undertook the chapters on some headmasters. Where this was unsuccessful Marilyn filled the gaps herself. Some chapters may contain "factual" errors, and some grammatical errors. If that should be the case then we sincerely apologise.

Leanne Baker was one of the first girls to go through the school. I first met her, late in October 2007. Although we had been in e-mail and telephone contact for over 2 years, her experience of publishing for her first employer (Derek Latham – Architect) was the injection of energy, enthusiasm, and know-how which turned the many hours of compilation and editing into an actual book.

It is my pleasure to thank Marilyn, Leanne, the many contributors, School staff, and finally Peter Newberry of Moorleys (our printers) all of whom have encouraged me to continue when the going has become uncertain. In the event it fell to me to be the editor. The text alone, without photographs, amounts to over 50,000 words.

On a personal note I have dedicated the book to my class-mate Stan Tacey. He was the first person to read the text and he assured me that it must be published. We were typical former pupils who went straight into work. Thanks to our education we made our way into "management". Stan used his talents to become an active member of Derbyshire County Cricket Club as the scorer. As a prolific writer for the Bygone pages of the Derby Evening Telegraph his command of English was due to his ability to learn from such teachers as Arthur House and Norman Clay.

Personally, I became involved in swimming, and even as I approach my 90th birthday I still swim when I can. I taught swimming, administered it and was an international official.

Old Bemrosians made their contributions in countless other ways. Perhaps someone will eventually produce a comprehensive account of their achievements both in working lives and in "hobbies" pursued. Every time I see James Bolam on the "box", fly British Airways, or walk into Boots, where Nigel Rudd was Chairman; I am reminded of what "our School" did for us to help us use our talents to the best of our ability.

Along with most Old Bemrosians, I take this belated opportunity to thank all the staff for their skill and devotion over the years, which enabled us to reach our full potential.

Old Bemrosians will read the book with pride and fond memories. New pupils will, I hope, find inspiration. Other readers will realise what an excellent school it was our privilege to attend. It is my hope that present day pupils will become just as proud as we are to say "we went to Bemrose School".

NOTE!
As the text of this book consists of contributions from a number of sources there is inevitably a mixture of styles of presentation.

PART ONE: BEMROSE SCHOOL FOR BOYS 1930 - 1975

CHAPTER 1

ORIGINS OF THE SCHOOL

Joseph Lancaster is credited with the start of education in Derby when he set up the British School in Orchard Street in 1811. By 1840 more schools had been built with two departments, one for boys and one for girls, providing inexpensive elementary education for the children of Derby.

By 1887, the Derby School Board controlled public elementary education in the town. They wanted to provide a more advanced type of education for the older children, resulting in the creation of the Higher Board School in Gerard Street, Derby. In 1891 this had an average attendance of 500 boys. Elementary education was by then free for all children.

The evolution and development of education is reflected in the social history of the last 100 years. At the turn of the 19th century post-elementary education was reserved for the privileged classes and self-improvement was viewed with suspicion by employers.

Balfour's Education Act of 1902 required Local Authorities to make provision for secondary education. It established the framework for advanced schooling. Council education committees, which eventually became Local Education Authorities (LEAs), were required to provide secondary schools in their areas, offering an academic curriculum and providing for pupils over and above the normal leaving age. Thus the Derby Municipal Secondary School for Boys and Girls (DMSS) was founded in Abbey Street School.

Abbey St School in 1970s

Abbey St School pictured during demolition.

The DMSS had a blue and gold uniform carrying the Derby insignia of the "Buck in the Park" a stag encircled by railings and a heraldic laurel. The School motto was "Per Ardua ad Astra" now familiar as that of the Royal Air Force. It was opened on October 12th, 1902 with Mr W G Constable as Headmaster of the boys' school with 8 masters and 76 pupils. The school was organised around a house system, with four houses named after great Englishmen: Newton, Sidney, Burke and Wellington.

Derby Municipal Secondary School, Form 1, 1904

When Derby Education Committee took over from the old School Board in May 1903, one of its first concerns was for the Abbey Street School to be recognised as a secondary school. Two officials from the Board of Education arrived from London and a sub-committee was formed to plan an overall scheme for an educational ladder in Derby – Abbey Street School would provide secondary schooling for both boys and girls, leading on to University or Technical College.

Abbey Street School was to be used for the training of teachers, who must be University graduates or have special qualifications approved by the Governors. (It is interesting to note that we have come full circle, Bemrose Community School today is an accredited Training School.) The new school should not unduly compete with other existing schools, such as the old established Derby School.

By 1906 there were 230 boys on the roll, but in February 1908 Mr Constable complained that some pupils stayed for such a short time that they could not benefit from secondary education and so it was decided to lower the age for scholarship winners to 11-12 year olds, and the parents had to agree to the child staying at school for at least 3 years.

W G Constable, first Headmaster 1904-1923

Secondary Education in 1911 cost £6 6s 0d a year at a Council School, but a percentage of free places were awarded on the result of a scholarship examination. Each year, Derby awarded scholarships of £4 per annum to 10 boys, and the local Co-operative Society granted an additional scholarship to a boy whose parents were Co-op Members.

In 1917 the girls' school moved to Parkfield Cedars, but the boys had to wait another 13 years before Bemrose School was opened on its present site.

In July 1923 Mr Constable retired and was succeeded by Mr W A Macfarlane.

The old school magazine for the Derby Municipal Secondary School was entitled "Demeses", the school logo was the Buck in the Park with railings and laurel wreath and the motto "Per Ardua ad Astra".

: DEMESES. :

The Magazine of the
Derby Municipal Secondary School for Boys.

Vol. I.   JANUARY, 1924.   No. 1.

EDITORIAL.

IT is obvious that a School like ours, active and increasing yearly in numbers and importance, should have its own magazine.

The DEMESES will serve as a permanent record of all School activities; and a glance through the following pages will show how numerous and how varied those activities are.

In presenting this, our first number, the Editors appeal to all School members, past and present, to make the magazine a great and permanent success. Remember that it is *your* work and *your* contributions and *your* subscriptions that will count.

We ask, therefore, that everyone interested in the School shall do his utmost to assist in the production of the magazine by writing articles, topical, sporting or educational; by sending in descriptions of things seen or heard, both in and out of School; and by writing original verse or stories.

In so doing, you will increase your share of, and interest in, the work of the School, and thus bring benefit to others as well as to yourself.

THE EDITORS.

VALE.

OUR former Headmaster, Mr. W. G. Constable, B.A., B.Sc. (Lond.), after a very long period of faithful service has now taken leave of us, but he will live long in the memory of many of the present boys, the Old Boys, and his former colleagues.

His chief work was in the direction of higher education, and to this task he brought a zeal and foresight which have left their impress on the life of Derby.

The School, of which he was the first Headmaster, is his immediate monument, and we may best perpetuate his memory by endeavouring to raise upon the foundation, which he has laid so well, a superstructure of which he will be proud.

Our late Head will ever be remembered by his conscientious devotion to duty, by his thoroughness, by his simplicity and modesty, and by his kindly influence and ever-ready help. At his hands shirkers received short shrift; but no boy who did his best ever failed to find in him a helpful friend and an encouraging counsellor.

Those who came into contact with Mr. Constable soon realised that the humorous side of school life always appealed to him,

The first school magazine
1924

SPEECH DAY

THURSDAY, MAY 16TH, 1929,

at 2.30 p.m., in the

CENTRAL HALL, DERBY.

DISTRIBUTION OF PRIZES

BY

THE REV. G. F. FISHER, M.A.

(Head Master of Repton).

CHAIRMAN :

ALDERMAN H. H. BEMROSE, M.A., Sc.D., J.P.

(Chairman of the Governors).

W. A. MACFARLANE, M.A.,

Head Master.

*The final
Speech Day
as
Derby Municipal
Secondary
School*

*Invitation
to the
opening
of the
new school*

Please present this Card.

The Chairman and Members of the Education
Committee invite the attendance of

Mr + Mrs Russell

at the

Opening of Bemrose School,

on Friday, July 11th, 1930, at 3 p.m.

by the

Rt. Hon. Sir Charles P. Trevelyan, Bart.,

P.C., M.P.   President of the Board of Education.

Entrance : Main Gate, Uttoxeter Road. Door IV. (to left of gateway).

Derby Municipal Secondary School's
Roll of Honour from World War I

The South Tower
Photos courtesy Andy Savage www.derbyphotos.co.uk

CHAPTER 2

HENRY HOWE BEMROSE, J.P., M.A., Sc.D., F.G.S.

Henry Howe Bemrose, JP, MA, ScD, FGS was the son of Sir Henry Howe Bemrose and a Director of Bemrose and Sons. William Bemrose came from a long line of Lincolnshire Yeomen. He moved to Derby in 1815.

He founded the printing firm Bemrose and Sons in 1826. Between 1855 and 1875 a major expansion took place as it pioneered lithography, colour printing and other techniques. During this time, one of its main contracts was printing timetables and other items for the Midland Railway. This continued in the 20th century after the railway amalgamation in 1922 when the Midland Railway became part of the London, Midland and Scottish Railway, the LMS.

William did not get involved in public life, but when he married Elizabeth, daughter of the Mayor of Derby, a whole network of municipal families joined together. One of their sons, also William (1831-1908), became Chairman of Derby School Board from 1896-1902. The Bemrose family had been interested in education since.

In 1857, Sir Henry Howe and Lady Charlotte Bemrose had a son, whom they named Henry Howe Bemrose. They also had five daughters. Henry assumed the name of Arnold to distinguish himself from his father of the same name. His admiration for Arnold of Rugby probably explains his choice.

Henry Howe Arnold Bemrose began his education at a Preparatory School at Spondon. His later studies were at Denbigh Grammar School where his aunt was married to the Headmaster Reverend J H Roberts who had previously been a master at Derby School. In 1875 he went up to Clare College, Cambridge as a Foundation Scholar in Mathematics. He gained his BA in 1879 and his MA in 1882 and settled at Lonsdale Place, Derby with his parents.

After graduating, Henry joined the family firm, which was situated at the bottom of Iron Gate in what is now Lloyds Bank and soon introduced the double entry system of book-keeping. In 1891, the family firm was incorporated as Bemrose and Sons Limited. He was appointed Deputy Chairman of the Board of Bemrose and Sons Limited shortly after his parents died in 1911. The First World War imposed great strains upon Dr. Bemrose, and he was one of only two Directors remaining in Derby, and acted as Company Secretary for a 14 month period.

It was at a Geological meeting in Cambridge in 1880 that he met Ellen Hyde, daughter of the late Reverend John Hyde. They married 10 years later and lived at 56 Friargate. They had four sons: Karl (1893), Roderick (1896), Clive Esmond (1902), and finally John Maxwell in 1904. The family moved after Clive was born to Ash Tree House, Osmaston Road, Derby. Karl was killed on the first day of the Battle of the Somme in 1916. Roderick was awarded the Military Cross as a result of being in action but died from his wounds on 8th November 1918, only 3 days before the Armistice.

Cambridge County Geographies

DERBYSHIRE

by

H. H. ARNOLD-BEMROSE, Sc.D.; F.G.S.

With Maps, Diagrams and Illustrations

Cambridge:
at the University Press
1910

Henry was a confirmed pipe smoker, loved to tramp the hills in all weathers, usually wearing shorts, and often enjoyed a pint of ale at the Anglers Rest Inn, Millers Dale. He was an enthusiastic and pioneering geologist, concentrating on Derbyshire. With his wife, he wrote *The County Geography of Derbyshire*. He also wrote a chapter in the Victoria County History of Derbyshire. He wrote many articles and papers on Derbyshire history and geology and was elected a Fellow of the Geological (later Royal) Society in December 1886.

By 1903 he was showing an interest in local politics, being co-opted to the Museum and Libraries Committee. Subsequently he was elected to Derby Town Council, which he served faithfully for 35 years. Twice he became Mayor, and from 1910 onwards was an Alderman. His interest in Education, as a member of the Education Committee for the entire period and its Chairman for 15 years, was to lead to the honour of naming a school after him. He was also Chairman of the Higher Education Committee and Hon. Secretary to the Derby University Extension Society for 23 years.

Invitation to the laying of the Foundation Stone

Municipal Secondary School, Derby.

The Headmaster requests the pleasure of the company of

Mr and Mrs Russell,

at Elm Tree House, on Friday, October 26th, 1928, at 3.0 p.m, when the

FOUNDATION STONE

of Bemrose School will be laid.

1928 Foundation Stone
Photos courtesy Andy Savage www.derbyphotos.co.uk

In 1905 Henry was presented with the Wollaston Medal of the Geological Society of London. His paper on the comprehensive framework of the igneous rocks of Derbyshire was just one of a series which led to him gaining a Doctorate in Science of Cambridge University, for scientific contributions. Every student of Derbyshire igneous rocks is familiar with his papers.

He dropped the "Arnold" from his name as his public work and responsibilities increased.

He became a Freemason; was appointed a JP and was Chairman of the Derwent Valley Water Board for 22 years. He gave enthusiastic support to the Boy Scouts in Derby, becoming District Scout Commissioner in 1913 and County Commissioner in 1922. In 1926, to celebrate the Company centenary, he compiled "The House of Bemrose 1826-1926" a substantial volume requiring a great deal of research.

After several years in which he was occupied with business and civic affairs, by 1928 he was able to resume his regular weekly field trips. 'Walk with a purpose' was his advice to others. On April 18th he was one of a group that ascended Snowdon in the snow at the age of 73, wearing shorts as usual! In October he laid the foundation stone of the new school.

In 1931 aged 76 he retired from Bemrose and Sons after 51 years' service. Henry spent more time out and about in Derbyshire, being transported in a chauffeur driven car. Amongst his many finds was an erratic boulder of Eskdale Granite, which he transported from a garden in Derby to Bemrose School. He continued his geological interests in retirement, lecturing at University College, Nottingham on the caves of Derbyshire, and writing articles for Derbyshire Countryside.

In 1935 Dr Bemrose was made a Freeman of his native Derby, and also became Vice President of the Council of University College, Nottingham and President of the Geological Society of London. His continuing outdoor interests led to yet another appointment as President of North Midland Youth Hostel Association in 1934. Three years later Lord Baden Powell, the Chief Scout, stayed with him at Ash Tree House on the very special occasion of a visit to the Drum Hill Scout site at Little Eaton where he handed over the lease of the land. One of the buildings there is now named the Bemrose Centre.

With a substantial record of published works associated with his many achievements, he personified a vein of scholarly enquiry and concern which has persisted in each of the descendants of William Bemrose. He stood in a long line of public spirited Englishmen to whom the government of their schools has owed so much. In all his life's activities – as a businessman, public servant, and private individual – he had linked science with industry; in public service and in his leisure he linked science and the service of others.

His two sons, Clive Esmond Bemrose, OBE and Sir Max Bemrose and his daughter Eliza Eleanor continue to show an interest in the school which has become his memorial.

He died at Ash Tree House on 17th July 1939 in his 83rd year after suffering a stroke.

Henry Howe Bemrose – oil painting by Ernest Townsend, presented to Dr Bemrose in 1938

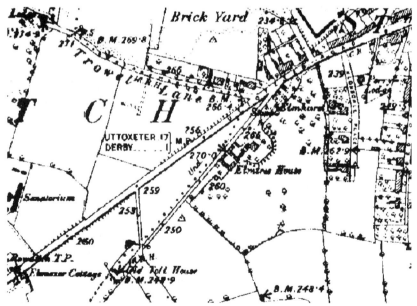

1887 Ordnance Survey showed the school site as Elmtree House

20

CHAPTER 3

THE BUILDING AND OPENING OF THE SCHOOL

The Elmtree House site on Uttoxeter Road was acquired in December 1923. It was purchased together with 18 acres of land. Pupils walked from Abbey Street to the Uttoxeter Road site for games from 1924.

The site was off the Rowditch, an old English name meaning "Rough Ditch" or Rughediche (1226). This was a small enclave astride the Rykneld Street Roman alignment, bounded by Bramble Brook, the Rough Heanor area of Mickleover and California. It does not appear in the Domesday Book, and is first named in a Charter of Burton Abbey, 1226. The focus of Rowditch is a small settlement where Uttoxeter Old and New Roads join. In 1819, the newly turnpiked Uttoxeter New Road diverged from the Old Road (Rykneld Street). A villa and a small group of houses, an inn and shops grew up around the resulting junction. A barracks with a drill square were created in 1859, but closed after barely 30 years. This has now become the Rowditch recreation ground, owned by the City Council, and there is a small park with tennis courts. Parcel Terrace was named after a parcel of land belonging to the settlement. Nearby, there was a railway line with trains from Derby Friargate to Tutbury and beyond, with a station at Mickleover. The line was used for goods traffic only from the late 1920s and closed completely after the war. This closure was before "Beeching".

The architects were Messrs Macpherson and Richardson, who submitted their drawings to the builders Gee, Walker and Slater in 1927. Plans were approved for a new building at a cost of £71,746. The school would be designed to accommodate 685 boys. Clerk of Works was Mr W Gregory and from April 1928 he worked on the building, until he presented the foundation stone. This was laid by Alderman Dr H H Bemrose, MA, ScD, FGS, JP - Chairman of Derbyshire Education Committee, who was accompanied by Arthur Sturgess, JP – Mayor - on 26th October 1928. In his remarks Dr Bemrose linked science and industry in the public service. The building would be a great opportunity for the teachers, and he was certain they would make good use of it. The new school was to be known as Bemrose School.

Many local contractors worked on the building. The ironwork was carried out by W H Haslam of St Helen's Street works, and the decoration by G Brailsford, painter and decorator of Cowley Street. The sanitary fittings were by Thomas Crump of Friar Gate. The now famous turret clock was manufactured and erected by John Smith and Sons of Queen Street, renowned clockmakers of international repute, their many clocks include the great clock in St. Paul's Cathedral. The building set new standards in secondary schools. Excellent lighting was one of the features, there being no fewer than 30,000 panes of glass in the building. Beautiful

Westmoreland slates were used for the roof, then said to be the largest roof of such slates in England. In addition to laboratories, woodwork room, library and refectory there was a well-equipped gymnasium.

On Friday 11th July, 1930 at 3.p.m. the school was formally opened by the Rt Hon, Sir Charles P Trevelyan, MP Bart, who was President of the Board of Education. The Chairman and Members of the Education Committee invited a distinguished audience, and the School Scout Troop provided a guard of honour. The school hall was so crowded that most of the boys listened to the speeches by means of loud speakers in the gymnasium and lecture theatre.

The Chair was taken by Alderman H H Bemrose. In a welcoming speech the Mayor of Derby Councillor J. Ferguson Bell said that Bemrose School would set a new standard for secondary schools; it was in a delightful situation and the boys who would work and play there began with every advantage. Alderman Bemrose, in seconding, spoke of the great strides that education had made, commenting that the child was the subject of greater study than ever before.

Opening Day with Mayor Councillor J Ferguson Bell delivering his address.
From Derbyshire Advertiser, 18th July 1930

Sir Charles Trevelyan had been struck by the airiness and lightness of the rooms and by their adequacy. He was pleased with the fine refectory and with the excellent stage. The surroundings of the school were indeed beautiful.

*Officials and dignitaries on the platform, with the boys in the Hall at the Opening
Ceremony – from an original photo by W Winters, loaned by Mrs P Bloor – whose
husband along with his brother are amongst the boys.*
Electronic image courtesy Andy Savage www.derbyphotos.co.uk

*Sir Charles P Trevelyan, President of Board of Education, with the Mayor,
Head Master W Macfarlane and Dr H H Bemrose.
Photographed by Derbyshire Advertiser at the opening.*

He had three wishes for the school. First, that it should be kept a school for all classes of the community, not merely because there were as good brains in the cottage as in the castle, but because boys ought to know no class distinctions. Secondly, that it would provide for every type of mind. Third that the school would produce good citizens.

He then declared the school open.

The school motto was 'Non Fallunt Merentem', meaning "The future does not let down he who merits it" and 'Non Nobis sed Allis', "Not for us but for others" was used for the 6th form.

School colours were changed from blue and gold to maroon and white. The "buck in the park" logo was no longer surrounded by railings. The house system was continued, with each having around 100 boys under the charge of a House Master, House Captain and Prefects.

Two new houses were added - Nelson and Gainsborough. The six houses were:

Burke *Motto* "Nil nisi bene" meaning "nothing except good."
Gainsborough "Unita Fortier - united we are stronger."
Nelson
Newton "Consilio et animis - thought and courage."
Sydney "Animo et fide - courage and loyalty."
Wellington "Pactum serva - do not break your word."

The laboratories were named after famous scientists: Faraday, Einstein, Ramsay, Berzelius, Pasteur, and Dalton.

In 1930, the school magazine was renamed "Bemrosia", the logo simplified to the Buck, and the motto changed to "Non fallunt Futura Merentem".

Staff and Pupils 1932

25

CHAPTER 4

W A MACFARLANE, 1930 – 1951

William Alexander Macfarlane MA
– Headmaster 1923 (DMSS) - 1951.

W A Macfarlane was born on 29th September 1888 and educated in Liverpool (1895 – 1907). He went on to Wadham College, Oxford to read Classics, becoming a prize winning scholar, and leaving with MA in 1912. He then spent 2 years at Liverpool University to obtain a Diploma in Education in 1914, before joining the staff as "Assistant Master" at Liverpool Collegiate School.

He left in 1923 to take up the post of Headmaster of Derby Municipal Secondary School (Abbey Street) in September 1923, at the then very substantial salary of £600 p.a., some 7 years before the move to the new School. His application included "Assistance is given in the teaching of Classics". Sarfas was to find in 1933 that this really meant he liked to teach a handpicked group of 12 who, by their prowess in Latin, should not find it too difficult to learn Greek.

W A Macfarlane in 1932
Photo from
Derbyshire Advertiser

A tall, over-weight, ponderous man, he was a formidable figure, giving an almost majestic outward impression of being stern, rather humourless and rarely relaxed. Some felt that underneath this veneer was a kindly and considerate man. A few might even have revered him! Not an easy man to know, he hated fuss and display. Universally known as "Mac" and later "The Boss" he embodied the School's ethos of discipline and diligence. His devotion was outstanding. He gave a great deal and would not compromise by giving less than his best.

W A Macfarlane, MA (Oxon)
Headmaster 1923-1951

Although stern, he was never oppressive, however at Abbey Street he struck fear into Sarfas, a Prep Form boy, making the 8 year old almost incoherent. This surprised him so much he sought advice from Kate Smith who was the Prep Form Mistress, always called "Sir" in those days. Nobody has recalled injustice at his hands; indeed sometimes he would rebuke rather than punish.

At the New School with its long corridors, he prowled most days with a regular slow gait, as though on an inspection. A characteristic feature was that as he walked slowly around the school, he appeared to be whistling. He would pause at the end of a corridor with his hands under his lapels, or behind his back under his gown, apparently deep in thought as to his next move. This stance was often displayed at the morning assembly.

In 1932 he married, the Old Bemrosians giving him a present of Crown Derby China. The Macfarlanes lived on Albany Road, opposite the school. They had three children, a son and two daughters.

The birth of the son had an unusual impact on Sarfas who was then (1934) a Greek scholar. Sarfas was unfortunate enough to be "kept in" each afternoon to learn the lines of Euripides' Alcestis. Wife and child used to join 'Mac' for tea about 4.45 pm so if he was not dealt with by this time he had to wait. If so delayed, as a "train" boy, Sarfas did not get home until 7 pm. With homework to do, this made life difficult in the School Certificate year!

Sarfas recalls his last sighting of Macfarlane at a Gilbert and Sullivan Evening at the Grand Theatre during the War. He was in the "gods", whilst Mac and his wife were in the stalls. At the end of the performance, during the National Anthem, the couple climbed over the back of their seats and left to avoid the crush and catch the last trolley-bus to Albany Road. At long last Sarfas realised that Mac was just a normal human being after all.

Bob Lyndall recalls Mac's uncharacteristic lapse into benignity when he agreed to early release from school of those who had asked to go to an important Derby County fixture.

Mac died on 1st March 1953, having retired the previous year due to ill health. One comment in an obituary said, "His work and faith were like bells that chimed together".

HUGH PRICE
- a former head boy, remembers the Macfarlane era.
It must have been a busy and exciting time during June 1930 when over 550 boys and the entire teaching staff including the incomparable Miss Smith from the Prep, Monty Brewster and Jerry Shaw (lab. technicians), and office staff moved from the dark Victorian Abbey Street site to the imposing light and airy Neo-Georgian new building on Uttoxeter New Road, on the edge of the town, and just within the

newly built ring road. It was not unfamiliar to the pupils as they had been visiting the site for football and cricket for some years.

Busy is certainly the word for July, for in rapid succession came the formal opening of the school, five days later the Hobbies Exhibition, and the following day came Speech day.

Speech Day 1948

The first edition of *Bemrosia* the renamed school magazine, gives an impression of everybody buckling down and beavering away at the same old curriculum, in which Latin was then, as for many years onward, an essential for Matriculation.

Hobbies Exhibitions have always been a big feature in the life of the school, and this 1930 show sounds pretty impressive, occupying the Art room, Hall, Chemistry and Physics labs, Gym and Handiwork room. The School Scout group had a display of their own in the gym. An unusual feature of the Hobbies Exhibitions was a performance of a Greek Play. This must have been something of a trial for the great majority of families, if not for the performers. Other features that carried on down the years were a choir contest and elocution, the latter much needed by those who sought to iron out the basically uncharming local accent. It comes as a surprise that prizes were awarded for hobbies, a competitive element that might well be frowned on today.

Hobbies Exhibition 1948

Pupils

Most came from within the Borough. The rest from as far afield as Willington, Repton and Melbourne as well as from the nearer villages such as Ockbrook and Borrowash. They came largely through the "Scholarship" system of selection, from so-called elementary schools, church or local council-run, which had in most cases been established in the 1870s after the first Education Act (Norvill taught us that!). Their parents probably had no more than the basic 3Rs education, so that they were amongst the last generation of children whose parents couldn't help them with their homework. It seems to have been possible for one's parents to pay the fees; starting at a little over £2 per term for the Prep. If one's grant for education didn't come up to the school's demand, then parents could make up the difference. And how did they get to school? In 1932 the magazine did a survey which showed that around 25% walked, 25% cycled and 50% got there by bus or train. No later figures are available. A pity - it might be interesting to compare with 1942 or 1962.

Hobbies Exhibition 1932

At least they had plenty of room, the school being designed to hold 600, but by September 1931 there were 662 of them, so the beginnings of larger classes had begun and never were easily overcome.

School Trips

Easter 1930, on the brink of the school move, there was a trip to Paris, and the same city endured a visit at Whitsuntide 1931. At Easter of that year there was an "old-established school event", a journey to Belgium based on Bruges, by 20 boys and 3 masters - a repeat visit is recorded in 1935.

Cruising seems to have got going in 1932 with a visit to Gibraltar, Morocco and Lisbon; in 1933 a Scandinavian cruise, including Hamburg and the Keil Canal and in 1935 another Norwegian jaunt. This time aboard the SS Nevasa, presumably not the grand air-conditioned liner of the same name which served as a troop-ship in the 1950s?

Similar voyages are recorded in later years, and land journeys to the continent - most surprising of all in late July 1939 - with war looming, a small group under Mr Slater went overland to Geneva! That must have been the last time any boy voluntarily went into Europe until after 1945.

Unusual Sports

Some pre-war activities are not usually associated with Bemrose School. Rugby football was being played, without much success, in the early 30s - apparently with much encouragement from Mr Blake who as an Irishman would have had more affinity with the oval ball. It seems to have dropped out of the news by 1939 and was never a serious contender for youthful energy. Somebody in 1931 wrote that "a school of 600 boys should be able to play soccer and rugby" but it just wasn't so.

Rowing too was an exercise that disappeared in those busy years, though in 1932 the Old Bemrosians were congratulated on a success (unspecified) in the Derby Regatta. Derby School of course persisted on the water, but they were much nearer the Derwent than the Bemrose hill. A rowing club was resurrected in 1951.

Boxing has been regularly recorded right up to 1939, organized mainly as an inter-house competition, supplemented by exhibition bouts from local professionals of the time. One scholar, a lad named Dolby, did himself become a pro, but this must have been very much an exception to the norm.

Bemrose School First XI Cricket Team in 1948

Back row;	Front:	Seated:
1. Mr Thornton (Cricket Master)	1. Peter Holland	1. Wilkinson
2. ??? (Scorer)	2. ???	2. Mayo
3. Jim Lingard	3. Philip Langridge	
4. Les Milton	4. Hugh Price (Captain)	

Scouts

Scouting doesn't seem so popular today, but in the inter-war years it blossomed. The old Abbey Street School had its own troop. In 1930, the 55th Derby Scout Group was started, run for the first 4 years by Mr H J Davis, an English Teacher who had run a Scout Group at his previous school in Ripon.

They went off to annual camps, the first in 1931 near Ripon. Meetings were held on Saturday mornings, and they found "plenty to do" at Drum Hill, the Scout Centre near Little Eaton.

After the 1932 Hobbies Exhibition there was a comment about their "astounding versatility" and later that year they paraded in Nottingham to see Lord Baden-Powell the Chief Scout. There is also from this year an admiring comment about rope-spinning display by Don Potter, later a prominent lawyer in Derby and a public official in the County. At some time this year the troop resolved (shades of things to come!) to "try for the Airman Badge". The Summer Camp was a few hundred yards below the Derwent Dam, just north of the now long-submerged Derwent village where Derwent Hall was a Youth Hostel. It was supported by several members of staff - Messrs Clay, Dauncey and Billy Lord. Davis was a power in the early days of the YHA with summer camps near Youth Hostels. In the next two years Overton Hall near Ashover, and Ilam were visited, perhaps showing some instinct toward security. The last pre-war camps in 1938 and 1939 were at Kibblestone in North Staffs. At the last one, 4 scouts achieved an unusual distinction by sleeping in the tree tops.

In 1935 they acquired their own Scout Hut which must have made them feel more independent; in the late summer there was a successful camp near Llangollen.

Mr Davis left to become Headmaster of Whitby School in 1934. Mr F A Cashin took over but left in 1936. Sadly the group seems to have disbanded with the call-up of the Scout Master during the War.

Old Bemrosians

The School passed fairly serenely through the 30s, with a slight but steady increase in numbers, particularly and - to the Headmaster gratifyingly - a bigger VIth form. More moved on, with State, Borough or County Scholarships, to University, some to Oxford or Cambridge and many more to the Redbricks.

Unsurprisingly nothing is recorded of failure at University, though Donald Locke, School Captain 1930-31, died aged 21 while still an undergraduate at University College, Oxford.

Most of the professions, including Architecture, found successful, even famous recruits, but sadly we can find no evidence of anyone rising to real eminence in the Church.

Local and National manufacturing and engineering firms, Government Agencies and other organizations trawled the school for talent; inviting or receiving groups of lads to see for themselves what was being done. Sometimes the Hobbies Exhibition was helped with displays by such organizations as the Gas Works and the opticians Lancaster and Thorpe. A late but typical example is Brian Summers who was beguiled into the Ordnance Survey after a visit in 1944.

Among the mid 30s exam successes and prize-winners is the name K O Warner, who became a quiet, unostentatious but much respected and long serving Family Doctor in Alvaston.

Some students were adventurous in their choice of career. Others perhaps understandably influenced by somewhat deprived backgrounds played for safety. Of these perhaps one of the most successful was George Emery, who after a hat full of School Prizes in 1936, and later the School Captaincy, entered the Civil Service. He admits that it looked to be "a secure if in some eyes a somewhat dull career at what was a difficult and gloomy pre-war period". He beavered away at various Ministries, at one time taking care of Hugh Gaitskell, and in 1980 retired with a CBE and an entry in Who's Who. A colleague of George, from the same Greek class, was John Stephen Hallet (Josh) White, who was also a civil servant, although not quite so eminent.

Sports

Football was overwhelmingly the most popular school sport, and first XI players were heroes - though one doesn't remember any great enthusiasm for going to watch them perform - games against other schools being almost always at weekends. Most sides were beatable, though people like Swanwick Hall were always tough - perhaps it was the mining background of their players.

Bemrosia regularly commented on the talents, and sometimes on the shortcomings, of the teams inevitably without being able to give much indication of the style of play. Bill Smellie coached for many years, and was hugely proud when in the early Post-war Years Tony Hull gained a Cambridge 1949 Soccer Blue. George Dixon, also a very fine cricketer, played in at least one English University Soccer side. In December 39 *Bemrosia* noted "an exceptionally gifted young player" and well they might, for this was Tommy Powell, later to become possibly the finest of Derby County's home-grown talents. Small wonder that Rugby never really caught on. However a revival took place with the arrival of a Welshman Danny Rees and is referred to in Chapter 11.

One of the stars of late wartime soccer was Phil Starkey, athlete and gymnast extraordinary, who was at one time playing for the School on a Saturday morning and for an adult competitive side in the afternoon.

He was succeeded by the hyperactive Don Woodruff, later a teacher. He played a large part in the School's huge post-war success on the field. Sadly his enthusiasm for fitness, especially in running, led in the end to two replacement hips and an early death, attributed largely to his anti-arthritic drugs.

School Plays

An annual affair, usually just before Christmas, the School Play was always well attended both by boys and families. Mostly Shakespeare, of course, though Bob Lyndall - a pre-Bemrose student - remembers a production of *The Knight of the Burning Pestle* at the old Temperance Hall in Curzon Street in 1929. The choice of play reflected the English Literature choice for the School Certificate Examination. In 1932 a special matinee of *The Tempest* was staged "for the unemployed of Derby". *(The time of the previous Great Depression before the credit crunch of 2009. Ed)*. The producers were members of Staff, Mr Freeman and Mr House until 1934, then Mr Downing until the War, followed by others until the arrival of Miss Olwen Jones.

The cast lists of most plays are worth a look. December 1931 saw Lewis Meakin as Osric. Meakin became a leading local journalist and somewhat feared as a drama critic.

The Henry IV in 1933 and Macbeth in 1934 saw the emergence of Leslie Drury, later to be Head Boy; he went on to a Science Degree at Liverpool, then wartime service as Royal Signals officer at El

School Plays "The Winter's Tale" 1950 and "Who Killed Cock Robin?" 1949

Alamein, and after a successful and inventive career in Commercial Engineering, emigrated to New Zealand in his late 80s in 2004.

A Midsummer Night's Dream in 1936 brought to the stage Snug in the shape of one J T Clewes, a prominent Derby Citizen often now seen about the Cathedral and a prominent Freemason. It was also the first recorded appearance of Eric Lander, as a fairy; he progressed to much greater things, playing Portia in 1939 and later found national acclaim as a television actor. The report on *The Merchant of Venice* opined that he "should have been born an Elizabethan".

Plays continued throughout the War but are not very well recorded. At the March 1941 Hobbies Exhibition there were four plays, one a Latin play by Form 1. 1944 saw the first appearance of the Bemrose Players, co-opting girls from Parkfield Cedars and Homelands, in a very stylish and well received production of Shaw's *St Joan*.

The 1945 "more elaborate than usual" production by Claude Gibson was marked by two things. First was the enforced appearance as substitutes (due to illness) of Mr House and Mr Gibson himself at very short notice. Second was the versatility and future potential of the original cast who became an Irish Barrister, an Accountant to the London Theatrical World, a Surgeon, a Consultant Rheumatologist, two General Practitioners and at least two Dentists.

The second and last Bemrose Players production was two years later, when the powerful Leonard Ashton played Macbeth in a production by George Hemmings; the latter a deeply studious man who after graduating from Nottingham returned to the School as a Member of Staff in 1949.

The scholars became more adventurous in post-war years, doing reviews and in 1951 a musical. *The Shrew* of 1947 saw the appearance of Peter Colston as Sly - later. Peter became a prominent manager in Rolls Royce but died early. Miss Jones soldiered on through these years as Producer until her last effort, a Middle School Revue in 1953.

Miscellaneous Comments

Just in case you should think that all was sweetness and light, it seems only right to record a few less reputable episodes in the School's history; no huge scandals, but definite blots on the record.

Bob Lyndall, a brisk and alert survivor from Abbey Street days, recalls that in the early 30s one OB, noted as a good performer in school plays, was imprisoned for fraud, having impersonated a member of the aristocracy.

In the late 40s another OB found himself inside, for activities which even in this liberal age remain illegal; and yet another of the same vintage found himself in serious trouble with his Professional Disciplinary Body.

Bad behaviour in School was rare and sporadic, but teachers with a poor disciplinary grip suffered badly. One such was Gwen Jelley, an inoffensive lady who came during the war years to teach Geography and was at times reduced to impotent rage by riotous larking about. She must have been greatly relieved when at the end of the war the gallant mathematician Alf Brown married her and took her away.

Another who had little or no grip, certainly on the lower forms was John Scupham. A Cambridge MA who taught English, he came in 1934 and was most successful with VI form classes, but juniors tormented him and he was often blackmailed into reading ghost stories to the class for the sake of peace and quiet. He left for a school in Cambridge in 1942 before finding an unharrassing niche at the BBC. Brierley (Ch.5) once met him there and, reminding him of his Bemrose years, drew from him a perhaps only half-humorous comment about "the dark ages".

Nobody has recorded personal bullying, that prominent feature of school stories from Tom Brown and Stalky & Co. onwards; but several individuals endured communal ragging or worse. Early in WW2 one Len Bonney (Bonsor in Brierley's account) was an outcast, frequently tormented and mocked, and sternly refused sanctuary inside the school by Monty Brewster, Lab Assistant, Gate-keeper and

General Factotum. Brierley rated Bonney as quite a talented writer, but unhappily he remained a figure of scorn.

Nussbaum, a continental refugee, always seemed a pleasant enough person but somehow didn't fit in. There was nothing racial or anti-Semitic in the ill-treatment he endured, but it was very real and obvious.

The worst sufferer, during the latter War years, was Moorcroft; not perhaps a particularly appealing character, he was on the receiving end of some quite spectacular gang violence, but it seems that he survives even now without physical disability.

Of course not everybody took an active part in this malevolence but sadly and shamefully nobody tried to stop it.

Post-War

By 1946 the School was at bursting point and some activities, particularly Handicrafts, were moved to pre-fab buildings in Albany Road. It would be many years before it was restored to the main school area in a large extension containing several facilities beyond the Geography Room.

January 1945 had brought the first entry of 13 plus boys. These were boys who had either "failed" or not taken the scholarship exam at 11 but were thought bright enough to be given another chance. John Raynes was one of these and has written a perceptive account of the problem of catching up after missing the first two years of Grammar School education. They were "a bit wild" and some teachers were intimidated, but they soon settled down. Some were remarkably successful, even though many were around 17 years old when taking the School Certificate Examination. Some "staggered into the VIth form" and in successive years Peter Colston and Raynes himself became School Captains. (See Ch. 10.)

*School Kitchen
1947*

A Class of 1947/8

Rear view of the school buildings, 1950, prior to the building of the tennis courts

37

Staff 1950

Back Row: Alan Pipes (Woodwork from 1947), Donc Dauncey (English from 1947), Horace Crossley (French 1931-50), Nobby Critchlow (Maths 1924-58), Danny Rees (PE from 1950), Carl Loeber (joined 1949 PE), George Hemmings (English 1949-58), Allan Goddard (French & Spanish from 1949), George Catton (Chemistry 1947-55), Bloxham (Biol & Chem), Alan Woods (Geog, married School Sec), Charles Dukes (aka Chisel Chukin' Charlie 1949-59), Squeaky Thornton (Maths from 1946), Pongo Molyneux (Maths & French 1945-71). **Middle Row:** Piggy Sowter (French & German 1948-72), Jack Mathers (Maths 1946-72), Basil Turner (Fr, Eng & Divinity from 1932), Billie Baxter (Chem 1920-53), Kenneth Eade (Music 1948-57).
Herbert Cook (Fr from 1948), John Trippett (Fr 1943-59), Ikey Watts (Art 1921-56), Monkey Maurer (Geog & Latin 1947-71), Bill Pickering (Eng 1935-73), Harry Harbach (Physics 1931-78), Larry Lamb (Biol 1947-55), W. R. Saunders (Metalwork 1949-66). **Front Row:** Killer Blake (Hd of Classics 1930-62), Mickie House (Hd Eng 1924-59), Major Smellie (Latin & Greek 1924-57), Crass Crowther (History & Latin (1915-52), W.S Spencer (Chem 1921-57), Nunky Norville (History 1930-65), Cuspy Raich Carter (Physics 1924-57), W.A. 'Mac' MacFarlane (Headmaster 1923-51), Kate Smith (Eng 1918-55), Polly Hepworth (Maths 1935-72), Elizabeth Hayward (Spanish 1950-55), Olive 'Clarabel' Jones (Eng 1945-58), W.J. Curly Pritchard (Maths 1940-55), Maurice 'Sammy' Severn (Geog 1946-72), Eric 'Sons' Branthwaite (Eng 1945-64).

CHAPTER 5

THE WAR YEARS, 1939-45

Six Old Bemrosians have contributed their recollections of the War Years. The contributors were Bill Grattidge (joined 1936), Peter Good (1939), Dennis Monk (1940), Robert Leighton (1940?), Alan Gifford (1940), and Ken Walters (1942).

The Civilian Scene in Wartime

Air Raid Precautions (ARP) were directed to protecting the population from the results of enemy bombing from everything except a direct hit. The "blackout" was an essential requirement, rigidly enforced by Wardens.

Express, Thursday, February 2, 1995   17

Constructing the Air Raid Shelters

At School sand bags were stacked in front of windows. Netting and sticky tape was applied to all inside windows to prevent flying splinters of glass. Other preparation for attack took the form of blackout paint to ground floor classrooms and the Hall. There was a blast wall constructed outside the main door. The Refectory became a heavily sand bagged First Aid Post, and the Hall was used for dinners as well as Assembly.

Air raid shelters were not completed until Easter 1940. Air raid warnings during lessons met with a drilled response. Pupils moved in an orderly fashion along the corridors to designated doors into a specific shelter. Peter Good recalls such an occasion: "We went to the appropriate underground shelter for our Form. No attempt at teaching down there, I suspect we sang. On leaving there were many vapour trails in the sky which we attributed to 'dog fights' with enemy aircraft".

Gas masks were carried at all times, and boys given detention if found without theirs. Eventually each entrance had roll down gas restricting curtains.

School Life

The school day was altered to 8.30 a.m. until 3.15 p.m. Uniform rules were relaxed, except for the School cap.

Sandbags protect the windows at Wartime Bemrose

Many of the male teachers were called up. These were replaced by women, the first being a Maths Teacher Mrs Tonkin. The reservation of the older men teachers meant that the school did not find itself depleted of Masters.

Most of the school playing fields were dug up to produce crops, the rest were "littered" with posts and old cars as a deterrent to landings of gliders or other aircraft. "Dig for Victory" produced vegetables for school dinners. Mr Heffer, the School Caretaker was in charge of teams of 30 boys who hoed, weeded, planted and picked, and many games periods were spent hoeing weeds.

Morning Assembly continued as usual. Mr Macfarlane included appropriate prayers on such occasions as the savage bombing of Coventry. This raid was one of the first "Baedeker" raids, so-called because Coventry Cathedral, almost completely destroyed in this ferocious attack, was listed in this German guidebook for tourists. The night sky was lit up by the flames and the effect was clearly visible from Derby which is some 35 miles away.

The Ministry of Information produced morale boosting films and books. *Target for tonight* was one of the first films. PG records compulsory attendance instead of lessons to see *The Battle for Stalingrad*. The books included one on the Coventry raid. It contained an account of how a goods train driver used his initiative to progress very cautiously past a red signal because the signal box was out of action.

Some lessons fell by the wayside, but woodwork classes took up a whole week each term. Pupils taking Latin but who were making very poor progress (Peter Good included) abandoned the subject and were given additional English Grammar lessons whenever Latin was on the timetable. Spanish was introduced instead of French, seen at the time as an "up and coming" second language.

During the period 1943/44 new students would be introduced into the class, in an attempt to find the appropriate level of tuition for them. Some would remain, others were moved. Some came from the Amber Valley temporary accommodation of Derby School, because of their inability to settle.

The School was enriched by evacuees and by a few refugees. Harry Kasriel, a German Jew who was genial and fitted in remarkably well, had great ambition "to make a million pounds" he once said, and after scholarship to LSE he became a prominent Economist. Klaus Jacoby, a refugee from Danzig, wrote in the *December 39 Bemrosia* a rather innocent but unself-pitying account of his journey from his home to the UK and eventually to Derby. A rather reserved man, he had a successful life as joint master of Raymond's News Agency - nursery and launching pad for many successful local and national journalists.

Some came from the South of England, notably Rubbra, related to the distinguished composer, and the Wood brothers, marked by their footballing power and strong London accents. A most interesting mix.

A more unusual activity was writing addresses on new Ration Books prior to their distribution by the Ministry of Food. At least one session was held in the Main Hall with its blacked out windows. Some pupils "blamed" subsequent troublesome eyesight on the poor light! Other Wartime activities included Christmas work at the General Post Office, Midland Road.

1940s view showing the grassy mounds of the air raid shelters

Digging for Victory

As mentioned above Mr Heffer was in charge of this effort to provide vegetables for school dinners. The success can be judged from the following record that in 1943 the school allotment of some 4 ½ acres produced:

7 tons Potatoes	4 ½ tons Cabbage	21 cwts Cauliflower
1x¾ cwt Celery	16 cwts Brussels Sprouts	18 cwts Carrots
17 cwts Onions	12 cwts Turnips	8x½ cwt Marrows
8x¼ cwt Parsnips	6x¼ cwt Broad Beans	5x¼ cwt Peas
5 cwts Beetroot	2x¼ cwt Parsley	1x½ cwt Lettuce
1 cwt Leeks		

In the summers of 1943 and 1944 the idea of allowing pupils to "help out on the land" was introduced. (Italian Prisoners of War were also employed in agriculture.)

Dennis Monk recalls that in Autumn there were many leaves to be collected for compost. These were bagged and carried in the Scout Group trek cart, which was also used to carry sacks of vegetables to the kitchen. The cart had been made in the school woodwork room. The Scout Group did not last long after the Scout Master went to the War, and anyway the Air Training Corps was more exciting. Incidentally, there was a pond in the playing fields, behind the Scout Hut, from where amoeba and other pond life were extracted for biology lessons.

Farming Camps

The first venue used to house pupils was Easton Hall near Grantham. Parties of about 30 volunteers were housed there in fortnightly periods, and taken by transport to nearby farms each day; some payment was received at the end of the fortnight.

Easton Hall Farm Camp drawn by Bill Goodchild

Always a sleepy station, Friar Gate, on the L.N.E.R. line was brought to life one Saturday in June 1943 by a crowd of Bemrose School boys and several prefects, about to embark on a new venture. As part of the War Effort, to enable the Country to be self-supporting, a fortnight's work "on the land" had been arranged by the School,

Kesteven District Council and the Ministry of Food. The base was to be an old manor house, Easton Hall, situated off the A1 about six miles from Grantham.

The majority of pupils had arrived on cycles, which were to prove an asset for use in the free time at weekends, and there may have been the idea of using them to get to a nearby farm, although the majority were transported by lorry. Everyone carried a small case with changes of clothing, and probably eating utensils. When the cycles were positioned in luggage vans, there was then a scramble for seats as the old rolling stock used by the L.N.E.R. had no corridors, and no means of interchanging if your best friend was in another compartment. PG coming from a railway family was used to train journeys, but these always began at Derby Midland Station. He was fascinated by the view as the train left Friar Gate, across the viaduct overlooking Brook Street on one side, and the gasometer in Cavendish Street, Willow Row and Cathedral Road on the opposite side. Moving on then to the Handyside Bridge across the Derwent, and the long-demolished bridge over Alfreton Road. The route continued to provide new scenery, and the sight of stations unknown to him at the time – Breadsall, Stanley, Ilkeston, Awsworth, Kimberley, and Basford until the memorable cavernous tunnels of Nottingham Victoria: but the train continued onwards to Grantham without the problems of changing. Bingham and Bottesford soon gave way to Grantham.

Once the cycles were unloaded, a line of schoolboys could be seen tackling the straight uphill road until the turn-off to Easton marked the near-completion of the ride; naturally it was a hot and sticky journey. Suitcases and haversacks followed in a vehicle which had been provided.

Eventually they were welcomed by the familiar face of Mr Carter (Senior Science teacher) and shown the sleeping quarters, a long room with wooden flooring, which must have been the ballroom for the Manor House. There was a glass conservatory at the far end, which housed about six sleepers. Simple straw-filled palliasses were placed directly on the unpolished wooden floor. The pillows provided were covered with their own pillowcases. The excitement of settling-in on the first night away from home meant that the jokes and talking continued for some time after official "Lights Out". There were no radios, no record players, nor even a piano, so the quick–witted provided the entertainment. Sunday meant further exploration of the area, a few games on the lawn, and the business of writing home, but with the apprehension of the work-day ahead there was less noise after "Lights Out".

Beyond the courtyard there was an archway supporting a little clock tower over the stables which provided dry storage for the cycles.

Meals were prepared in the original kitchens. Other teachers present, such as Miss Hough or Miss Higginson helped prepare the meals. A corridor from the dormitory led the pupils to a row of servers who dispensed the food on to the sectioned rectangular tray used by military establishments. Care was required carrying the assembled tray to a vacant seat, otherwise the unusual combination of meat and seats might occur. Whether boys were required to take turns in potato peeling ("spud bashing") or any details of the meals, does not come readily to mind. Being the middle of the war, many fruits were unobtainable, and the large caterer's tins of beans and corned beef provided basics with which to ring changes. Peter Good commented, "I never felt hungry".

Mid-day packs of sandwiches were also provided for the lunch-break on the land and these were devoured readily, clean hands or not.

"Sixty years ago there was not the pressure to wear long trousers, and every pupil turned out for work in shorts of some type or other. Having been designated to a particular work team, we were picked up by an open lorry, whilst there was still a nip in the air, and taken to the farm.

"The journey usually involved returning to Grantham, and then travelling northward into flat fen countryside. Possibly near Manthorpe or Gonerby, where hours of back-aching potato picking awaited our attention. A tractor tailing a spinner, which turned over the dying potato plants in their neat rows, brought to the surface an abundance of potatoes as it worked endlessly around the field. Weighing machines extended the length of the growing crops at intervals of about twenty yards; these were operated by regular farmhands, many of them women. The schoolboy helpers were divided between these groups, and using old wicker baskets were required to clear the ground of all visible potatoes, return with them to the weighing stations where they were bagged up in hundred weight sacks (112lbs) ready for storage, or the markets. Because the tractor was running on a circular route which diminished gradually, once one line had been cleared another 8 or 10 yards across the field suddenly became our urgent responsibility. There was little time to get to know the people with whom we were working, although this did develop, and we learnt that the relentless pattern of picking was because 'piece rate' payment was in operation."

Bemrose Schoolboys harvest turnips at a local farm - November 1940

There was a variety of work. Some were set to picking strawberries. "Eat as many as you like" they were told, but they soon became sick of that! Other work included singling sugar beet, pulling flax that had been flattened by wind and rain and couldn't be cut by the reaper, and thinning-out young carrot plants. A field can seem endless with such small growths in rows and was said to have resulted in "little green clusters which persisted before one's eyes long afterwards". During the fortnight there was some variation in work - clearing a barn on a damp morning. Others pulled watercress. The beds were narrow concrete troughs, the shallow water level being controlled by wooden sluices. The water was obtained from an artesian well. Yet another part of our education.

Sandwich break at midday was very welcome, as indeed was the sight of the lorry to take us back to Easton Hall at the end of the afternoon.

"One afternoon the weather must have been so bad that a crowd went to a film at the State Cinema in Grantham showing "Yankee Doodle Dandy" starring James Cagney. I learnt afterwards that it seated 1300 people, and was very full on the occasion of our visit. One of the popular songs of the time "You'd be so nice to come home to" was sung all over the Hall, even though everyone was enjoying themselves, and did not appreciate its wistful lyrics. My interest in cinemas was already established at that time, and I went to the Theatre Royal, also showing films, although pillars supporting the balcony marred the view in the rear stalls. Another, the Central, was obviously a public hall adapted as a cinema, filled with daylight from windows on both side walls, the curtains being drawn before the show commenced.

"On the second Sunday morning of the fortnight Mr Carter, a loyal Anglican, persuaded many of us to attend matins at Easton Church, which like many such was a part of the Estate. I cannot trace the name of the church, or whether it is still in use, but the congregation was swelled considerably. It had a number of box pews for exclusive use by the local gentry.

"The second week saw a relaxation in the acquaintance with the farm workers who naturally viewed us with some awe or suspicion. The work went on until suddenly it was time to pack, and following another noisy night, retrace our journey - vowing to enrol on the next fortnight available! I arrived home with about £4 as a result of my labours.

"At the Easter Camp in 1945, we were being brought back to Camp in the farmer's lorry, when we passed through Bourne, near Braceborough. There was an air of excitement and street decorations were being put up. Now every morning a Post Orderly was detailed to go to Braceborough Post Office to collect the camp post. The next day the Orderly came back with the postbag over his shoulder, riding his bicycle single-handed along a rutted track shouting, "The War's over! The War's over!" I believe it was Mr Carter that went to the Post Office to phone home for instructions. He came back saying we could all go home if we wished. I'm sure we all did, to join in the Victory celebrations."

Dennis Monk recalls one year, it must have been 1944, seeing RAF Typhoons loaded with rockets, flying to the Continent. On their return, empty, the boys gave them the V-sign by holding up two hoes and got a waggle of wings in return. A problem living in isolation was not receiving any War News on the wireless. He built a crystal set one year but reception was not very satisfactory, perhaps because of enemy jamming. The next year he built a more powerful two-valve set, but it needed batteries and again was not very satisfactory.

One night he was woken by noises outside, and found a mock battle taking place between soldiers on night exercise. On another night he was awakened by the sound of aircraft and looked out to find the sky full of aircraft and gliders. It might have been D-day or later the action at Arnhem.

680 Bemrose School Squadron Air Training Corps

Dennis Monk joined the ATC under age at 13 years; officially one had to be 15 years old. The Squadron met three nights a week after School. Mr Brown, Flight Lieutenant, was the Commanding Officer, and Mr Molyneux was Second in Command, perhaps Pilot Officer. They learnt drill on the Eastern Quadrangle. This stood Dennis in good stead when subsequently, during National Service, he had to march a squad of RAF personnel from Padgate to Warrington Station. "I had to stop them on the white line at traffic lights and give the 'eyes right' to a funeral." Ex ATC members were given an RAF Service Number prefaced by the numbers 313(4732) so that they could be identified.

"Other activities included learning the Morse Code, Aircraft Navigation, Aircraft Recognition, Aero-engine Maintenance and Repair and Rifle shooting. The latter used the LMS Railway Rifle Club Range in one of the old Pullman sheds on London Road. On several occasions we were taken by special Trent bus to Burnaston Airfield for "circuits and bumps" – take off, circuit the airfield and land.

We had to have a letter from our parents giving permission for us to fly and had to sign out and back at the control tower. We were kitted out with a flying suit and a parachute that formed a cushion on which one sat in the aircraft bucket seat. It wasn't easy walking with the chute strapped to us. The aircraft was usually a Tiger Moth twin seat open cockpit biplane trainer. Communication between pilot and passenger was by speaking tube.

On one occasion I asked if I could take the controls. "Take the stick, put your feet on the rudder bar" came the voice over the speaking tube. This done, he threw his arms in the air saying "You've got her". There was a sinking feeling in the pit of my stomach! I quickly recovered and was surprised to find how sensitive the aeroplane was to the controls. "Turn gently to port" said the voice and I turned in the direction of the airfield. The engine was cut to idling and we gently glided down. To my relief the voice said "I've got her" and we landed – I thought I was expected to try it!

"Another time I was flown by the Chief Instructor, in his Miles Magister. This was a twin seat low wing single-engine monoplane with a closed cockpit and also a trainer. We flew down the (old) Burton Road and over Rolls Royce. The pilot cut the engine to idling so that I could hear over the speaking tube, and banked the aircraft to point to Rolls Royce with the starboard wing tip, saying 'that's Rolls Royce on the end of the wingtip - not very well camouflaged is it?' I thought to myself maybe, but we were only at 2,000 feet; what must it be like at 30,000 feet? We flew over Derby and back to Burnaston down Uttoxeter Road, over the School.

"Once we were given a navigational exercise. In the Briefing Room we were given charts, wind speed and direction, then had to work out vectors and plot our flight path over a triangular course turning over Blith Reservoir and perhaps over Lichfield. The aircraft was a Miles Dominie twin-engine biplane, seating seven enclosed behind the pilot. After the flights, the pilot signed out in the Control Tower, cycled across to the parked aircraft, put the cycle aboard, climbed in and flew off.

No 680 (Bemrose School) Squadron of the Air Training Corps
at RAF Honniley Camp in 1943

"Other ATC activities included attendance at various Service Parades to support National Savings Weeks, such as "Wings for Victory Week", when the population was encouraged to put its money into National Savings to support the War Effort. These took place on a Sunday and included Regular Service Personnel and cadets from all the Services. It formed up in the old cattle market and marched to Full Street, down Iron Gate to the Market Place, where some dignitary would take the salute to the Cenotaph. The 126 Rolls Royce Squadron had a band that led us. On one occasion there was a heavy shower of rain, which tightened and burst the natural pigskin used on the drums in those days, so that we finished marching to a single drumbeat.

"Further activities included memory drill - marching without commands - which I believe the ATC pioneered. We practised this drill in the Old Police Station Yard, by the side of the Magistrates' Court, for some weeks before the event. The demonstrations took place in the Market Place during the Savings Week and must have been during holidays. The ATC held an Annual Summer Camp at an RAF airfield, but I went to the Farm Camp, perhaps because it was more lucrative as we were paid for our work.

"Perhaps I should mention that during the War there was Double Summer Time, so that in Summer darkness fell about 11 o'clock at night. Later in the War during summers' evenings (1943 or 44), as darkness fell, we saw a stream of Lancaster bombers flying West at minute intervals to gain height, returning East at greater height, on their way to Germany. That lifted our morale!"

Social Occasions

Ken Walters remembers that in 1944 American soldiers injured in the Normandy offensive were hospitalized in the Sudbury area and before Christmas of that year Miss Smith appealed to all the school for any families which would be able to entertain one or two soldiers for Christmas Day. He writes, "Mother and Father agreed to offer hospitality and so it was that two American soldiers arrived by army truck on Christmas Morning to join in our festive meal and spend time with a typical English family. They stayed with us for the whole day, telling us about themselves and their family back home. In the evening we played the usual parlour games of that era like *Subject and Object* finishing up with a singsong which included such songs as *Bluebirds over the white cliffs of Dover* and *Coming in on a wing and a prayer* accompanied by Mother on the piano. Garvin Haist from Los Angeles and Robert W Kolts from Salt Lake City were really appreciative of the time they had spent with us and Mother kept up correspondence with them and their families for many years after the war. They even sent small food parcels to us during those difficult days of rationing.

"In my autograph album I treasure the two entries which they made:

> 'To a very, very swell English family who made a Christmas a long way from home almost as perfect as if I had been at home. Remember a G.I. who you made very happy.' Garvin Haist, Los Angeles, California, 5536 Marburn Ave.

> 'May your joys be as deep as the ocean and your troubles as light as its foam. Happy New Year wishes and hope you will have many more joyous Christmas days. With many thanks.' Robert W Kolts 2349So 13E Salt Lake City, Utah.

"The following Christmas we entertained two more GIs. They however only stayed for Christmas dinner then went off into Derby for their entertainment! Father was not too pleased.

"Kate Smith arranged a slightly longer break for some Australian airmen, two of them staying at my friend, David Cherry's house and one with us at our bungalow. We had a few very enjoyable days in each other's company, but David and I were still at school during the daytime and the airmen were collected and taken out for the day by other agencies. I remember getting into trouble with Father for not doing my homework one night because I had been down at David's all evening with all the three airmen. It was 408530 F/SGT Smith G.G. RAAF (Glen) who stayed with us. I little thought that years later I would be visiting that country to see my own daughter and her family after they emigrated to South Australia."

A Personal Account by Ken Walters (1942-50)

When I was 11, education was selective and all pupils in the final year of Junior School sat the "Eleven Plus" examination to determine whether one went on to Senior School, leaving at fourteen to start work, or to Grammar School for an academic career.

There was a hierarchy in Derby. Derby School, with their straw boaters and black blazers with a mitre shaped badge was at the pinnacle, then came Bemrose, sporting maroon blazers bearing the Buck in the Park on the pocket and caps quartered grey and blue. These were Local Authority Schools for boys. For the girls there were two schools, namely Homelands and Parkfield Cedars.

I well remember my father filling in the form requesting the order of choice of school. At that time Derby School was evacuated to Amber Valley and Mother did not want me to leave home so Bemrose became first choice followed by Central and finally Derby School. As a result I continued my education in the September of 1942 at the school of my first choice, Bemrose School for Boys, to give its full title or "Bemrose Bucket Bangers" as it was nicknamed by boys from other schools!

September 1942 saw me assembling along with all the other new boys in the open area at the East End of the School under the scrutiny of a gentleman wearing what looked to me like a Doctor's White Coat, I was sure we were in for a medical examination! However it turned out to be "Monty" Brewster, the Senior Laboratory Assistant whose job that morning was to assist in marshalling the new intake of eleven year old boys, which I suppose must have numbered about 120.

We must have looked a colourful sight in our brand new uniforms, mine purchased from Derby Co-operative Society, using their Mutuality Club scheme, which enabled Mother to spread the initial outlay over a period of time. I was still wearing short grey trousers, as were most of the boys of that age in those days.

As we were called out to our classes, we entered through a double door at the side of the building into what must have been the Library, but it was so dark inside and before I could find my way I was grabbed by several older boys who propelled me across a highly polished floor. I feel this was a prank which Sixth Formers had been indulging in on previous intake days! This was the only time I experienced this form of treatment during my time at Bemrose.

It was a four stream entry and each class had its identity. Starting with 2.1, my class, then 2.2 followed by 2.3 and 2.4, the latter two classes taking Latin as an extra language subject, so you can guess who the bright boys were!

My first Form Teacher was Margaret Higginson, a lovely lady with ginger hair, freckled face and always immaculately dressed. I am not sure how long she had been teaching but I think we tried her patience at times.

We were a very mixed bag and from very opposite ends of the social scale. I was neither a scholar nor an outstanding sportsman, but my first report at the end of the Autumn Term seemed to suggest that I had worked reasonably hard and was a fairly accurate prediction of my final results. I only received C for Maths, which I was to fail at School Certificate and A for Manual Instruction i.e. woodwork, which I eventually followed in my career.

The first Assembly of the day for the new boys took place in the Lecture Theatre and was addressed by the Deputy Headmaster, Mr Carter, shortly to be known as "Raich" complete with blue and white spotted bow tie. The only part of this which I remember was his description of the plan of the School as being like the Greek letter π (pi), which is no longer the case now the new glass structure has been grafted on. I am sure that he must have introduced us to the various rules of the School, one of which was that the stairs at the East End were for ascending and those at the West End for descending and there were always prefects on duty to see that this was adhered to. It certainly made life easier as 800 boys had to change classrooms several times during the day.

The building had been well prepared for the War and played its part by housing an ARP Post in what was the refectory but later became the Library, as this part of the building only became used by pupils after 1945. In my early days the Library was housed off the first floor corridor together with Nunky Norvill's history room, the art room and Nunky's sixth form room. Sandbags protected all the entrances and the large windows on the South Side of the school were blacked out with paint and curtains. We spent a lot of time in artificial light. There were concrete air raid shelters along the bank at the West End but I can not remember entering them at any time during the War. It was a real eye opener when, after three years of working in these conditions, the School was opened up to daylight and the Library was returned to its proper use. The refectory became the Library when the new extension to the west was built.

What a change from the Junior School I had left. Here there were large classrooms, specialist laboratories for chemistry, physics and biology, rooms for art, woodwork, geography and a very well equipped gymnasium. The Hall was awe inspiring to me with its curtained stage and balcony and capable of accommodating 800 boys for Morning Assembly. The Headmaster, Mr Macfarlane, would make a dramatic entry from stage right, his black gown flowing behind him ready to begin Morning Assembly starting with a short service. If the assembled masses were not as quiet as he liked he would stalk off and the Housemaster in charge of the Assembly then had the task of bringing everyone to order before the Head made his appearance once more. Discipline was firm and effective!

One of the first difficulties I encountered was the taking of notes during lessons. At the Junior School I had never used joined script and so I was still printing and this made the task much slower for me than for many of the other boys. I very quickly had to learn how to join letters together and the result is that even today my handwriting is not good.

School meals were the other big change for me, since I had always been able to go home during the two hour lunch break, which was common in those days. Meals were served in the Hall, boys sitting eight to a table. After a Latin grace, led by the Headmaster and which I never understood or even managed to get my tongue round, the food was brought round on trolleys to each table. The Table Captain, usually a Sixth Form boy, then dealt out the meal from tureens and served each member of his table. Fair shares for all seemed to be the order of the day but there must have been some unscrupulous table captains! To ensure the smooth running of the meal, Jerry Shaw, the Junior Laboratory Assistant would race round the hall like someone demented. I believe he went on to become a teacher eventually. One thing I am sure about and that is that my first table captain in 1942, Gordon Hemmings, a rather shy, academically minded boy was back at Bemrose in 1950 as a member of staff, because he is on the school staff photograph of that year.

The other activity, which took place in the Hall, was our music lesson with Mr Fitch, who, with the aid of his grand piano, endeavoured to instil some knowledge and enjoyment of his subject into a class of non-receptive pupils. He moved about very quickly and as a result the lower part of his gown was shredded in ribbons because it was always getting caught in the doorway as he dashed through! I should be eternally grateful to Mr Fitch since it was he who organized a Concert by a French singing group called "La Faluche". I was asked by a girl at my church if I would take her to it, which I did, things developed from there and in 1953 Nora and I were married, celebrating our Golden Wedding last year!

Speech Day was a highly ceremonious occasion held in the Hall and with all the staff wearing their many different University Hoods. It was a colourful sight. The Headmaster and dignitaries assembled on the stage and after an introduction by the Head the Main Speaker would deliver his words of wisdom to us. Then followed the prize distribution, this included House Awards of shields and cups along with individual book prizes for different subjects in each year. I was extremely proud to be able to return in 1951, wearing my army uniform, to receive a prize for Handicraft. Prior to one such event Mr Macfarlane had the School assembled and gave a rather terse lecture on the importance of not appearing bored by the speech making, even if you were! Whether he knew that the speaker was to be uninspiring I don't know but that talk has always stuck with me. I feel it was part of the social education, which Bemrose provided and which started with the large banner one saw on entering Miss Smith's classroom. It read "Manners Maketh Man".

On starting at Bemrose I was amused to find that the female members of staff were addressed as "Sir". This must have been a relic from the days before the War when the Staff was all male, although Kate Smith had taught the fee-paying Preparatory Class since 1924. At Morning Assembly Mr Macfarlane informed the whole School that henceforth the term "Madam" would be used when speaking to female staff.

On another occasion, at the end of Morning Assembly, Mr Norvill, in a very serious tone, requested that the ladies withdrew and then proceeded to inform the school that boys had been leaving empty milk bottles in the toilet area. This was a practice which must cease forthwith. He was in charge of milk distribution!

Science was always fascinating, especially during the lesson when Mr Spencer wrapped a small piece of sodium in some wire gauze and casually dropped it into a large cylindrical glass bowl filled with water. It was supposed to travel across the water like a boat. Instead it sank to the bottom and the bowl split into two neat halves depositing the water all over the bench and on to those boys at the front who were eagerly watching the experiment! "Oh dear," said Mr Spencer, "I must have trapped some air inside the gauze."

Physical Education during my time was in the hands of Mr Habib, a Middle-Eastern gentleman who had studied at Loughborough College and was reputed to be a champion fencer and the scars on his face seemed to confirm this! I remember him trying to teach me how to do a handstand on the box. I managed to get myself into the vertical position and despite Mr Habib's support I collapsed in a heap on the mat below. I was never his star pupil. Nor was the lad from a farming family who did things rather casually. Mr Habib would say, "What you got in your head? Straw?"

Sports afternoons were not my favourite since I was never picked to play in a team for football and always finished up on the Lower Pitch with the "left-overs". I usually offered to stand in goal, as I could never kick the ball in a meaningful direction.

I was in this position one afternoon when a spitfire came zooming very low along the length of our pitch and I was so absorbed by watching this that the other team attacked and scored a goal. Imagine my popularity.

The Lower Sports Ground had been turned over to agricultural use during the War and George, the gardener, supervised gardening classes. I can only ever remember being part of a gang, which was required to drag an old iron gate over the ground to harrow it and also spend an afternoon laboriously hand weeding the crops. Where the results of our efforts went I have no idea.

Swimming Galas were held at the Queen Street Baths and were always occasions for inter-house rivalry. There were always impressive displays of diving, racing in the various swimming strokes and water polo matches. The noise 800 boys could make in that place, urging on their teams, was incredible. I suppose the loudest cry went up when a very well built Sixth Former named Lebeter, an excellent swimmer, made a belly flop entry at the shallow end drenching the headmaster and his guests, which included the Mayor and Mayoress of Derby, even though they were shielded by a plastic sheet in front of their legs.

Sports Day was another time when inter-house rivalry was evident and it usually took place on a Summer afternoon on the Lower Field where a quarter mile running track was laid out and with a 100 yard sprint track close to the bank where the spectators gathered. Field events such as javelin, discus, throwing the cricket ball, long and high jump went on all afternoon interspersed with track events, which concluded with the one mile race, four times round the track. The house scores were recorded on a blackboard and kept up to date for the onlookers.

The four houses referred to above were named after illustrious figures from History and were Burke under the command of Mr Crowther, Newton with Mr Norvill, Sidney with Mr Spencer, and Wellington, my house, managed by Mr Smellie.

The other main school event was the Annual Shakespeare Production, which I believe was initiated by Claude Gibson, but by my time Miss Jones had taken over as Producer. The two most notable performers were Leonard Ashton, who always played the female lead and a lad named Cox, who had such a wonderful deep voice and starred as the main character. The plays used the excellent stage facilities to their best advantage.

My journey to school started by walking from my home in Shropshire Avenue to the bus stop at Nottingham Road Cemetery. From there the number 60 trolley bus, from Chaddesden Park Road or the 66 from Nottingham Road Creamery took me to town where I went from the Market Place to Victoria Street to catch the 55 up to school. After a time, in decent weather, my friend, Roy Attwood, and I would walk through Sadler Gate and Cheapside then up Uttoxeter Road to arrive just before 8.55. On some occasions, Don Shaw would be on the 66 bus from Chaddesden and he would accompany us.

I did arrive late a few times and suffered the indignity of being confined to the cloakroom, under the eye of the Duty Teacher, until morning service was ended. Names were recorded in the late book and it was entered on the end of term report. Mine shows twice when I was in T20 and three times when in VIB Arts. I had become a rebellious teenager!

Punishment for severe misdemeanours was dealt with by caning but the more usual was detention after school. I avoided this until very late in my school career when I accompanied a friend to a dental appointment at the City Hospital. On return I was met in the corridor by a very irate Mr Macfarlane who informed me that it was John Bailey's parents who should have accompanied him not me. Mac was livid and his face went bright red, matching his hair, as he slapped his hands together to emphasis his point.

My only other encounter with Mr Macfarlane was after a rather disastrous first interview at Loughborough College, when I did not come over as a forceful enough person for their requirements. He called me in and told me what had been said and then likened an interview to a game of tennis saying that as well as returning the opponent's shots you had to be able to set up your own service. To a non-sportsperson like me this did not really mean much but I think I got the drift. At my next interview, after two years in the army, I was more forceful asking questions, the final one being "Do I have a place or not?" at which a bemused Mr Ockenden looked at his Colleagues for their assent and then said "Yes".

I think it was for my previous misdemeanour that I experienced my only detention. This meant going to a designated classroom and being supervised by a Duty Teacher whilst tackling a maths exercise suited to the age group you were in. As I had failed maths at School Certificate level and had dropped the subject on entering the sixth form there was very little I could do, so that at the end of the hour I was released after handing in a fairly clean piece of paper!

There was one other occasion when I handed in a blank sheet and that was when I sat a Latin examination. When I entered the Upper Sixth form my Form Master, Mr House, who was also careers master, advised three of us that we should attempt a crash course in Latin so that we could be in a position to apply for University entrance. Although we were set on becoming Craft teachers we started having lessons in Latin from Mr "Killer" Blake. It was he who always took the Roman Catholic pupils for their Morning Service and who could be viewed from the Playing Field having a game of cards at dinner time in the staff room with "Ikey" Watts the art teacher. He had a fearsome reputation as a disciplinarian but he treated us as adults and I think he was as much bemused by the situation as we were. At the Examination I filled in my candidate details, looked through the paper, decided it was beyond me to attempt any of the questions, and waited the requisite half hour before handling the blank paper to a rather concerned Mr Crossley. I then went and spent the rest of the morning in the woodwork room! I can still just about decline the verb 'to be!'

All the Members of Staff at Bemrose were excellent teachers; the only exception I can recall was the fellow who came to teach Biology after the War. We quickly learned that he would spend the lesson recounting his War experiences if we encouraged him to. I think he stayed a term.

At the other end of the scale was Mr House whose box analysis of exam papers was second to none. He could accurately predict which questions would come up that year and even advise which quotations to learn! The other thing about "Mickey" was that he was reputed to be flyweight-boxing champion of the Mediterranean Fleet and you did not mess with him. We repaired a dolls house in the woodwork shop one Christmas for his daughters.

Art with "Ikey" Watts was always a joy. He made even the inept artists capable of producing some worthwhile result, although I was glad when, for our class Life

Drawing Lesson he chose me as model and presented me with his drawing afterwards.

History with "Nunc" Norvill I found a bit oppressive. It was so full of facts and dates and his rather monotonous voice did nothing to keep me alert during the first lesson after lunch when attention was likely to wander.

On the other hand "Sammy" Severn brought geography alive for me. He was so enthusiastic especially with Physical Geography and Map Work and I still have an interest for that subject today.

Of all the English teachers I had it was Miss Jones who probably did the most to ensure I could write a reasonable essay. I am sure her method for tackling a piece of written work was unique and was so necessary for marshalling one's ideas.

Finally there was that ginger haired dynamic man with the high pitched voice who came just in time to ensure that I passed my Higher School Certificate French. It was Herbert Cook who arranged an exchange of pen pals and I corresponded with a boy in Dijon. Our letters to each other were returned, corrected so that we learned from our mistakes. I built up a fantastic collection of French stamps and in the Easter of 1949 I went off to France on my own and stayed with the family for a fortnight and learned French as the French speak it. I still keep contact and write every Easter and Christmas.

Manual Instruction was the heading on the end of term report to describe Woodwork, for that was the only craft available when I started at Bemrose. In 1947 the description was changed to Handicraft. The Workshop in 1942 was adjacent to the Gymnasium on the top floor at the East End of the school. It must have been above the downstairs cloakroom so the noise had been taken into consideration in the planning. In charge was Mr "Toddy" Howell assisted by a much younger man, Mr Ron Hanlon. Neither of them fitted the stereotype of craft teachers of the day, ex tradesmen who had qualified as craft teachers by the way of City and Guilds of London Handicraft certificate and who were alleged to hurl mallets about with gay abandon! Both wore immaculate white warehouse coats as opposed to the drab brown ones favoured by other craft teachers. Something I emulated when I began teaching.

At his retirement presentation Mr Howell graciously accepted a landscape painting and said that he would now have more time to read his Bible – a competent craftsman and a true gentleman.

I was in Mr Hanlon's group for instruction, and under his guidance over the next eight years I was to develop my skills as a worker in wood.

I can still see Mr Hanlon's assessment of our joint making efforts as he gathered us together by calling "Come round boys!" at which we would assemble around his demonstration bench for his verdict. He would then proceed to go through the pile with his comments and his skill in tossing those that did not come up to scratch into the waste box had to be seen to be believed. He was a jovial type of person and would often make jokes and on one occasion the joke was on me.

The class rogue had made some misdemeanour and was to be punished. Out came Ron's implement of torture … a two-foot long piece of leather machine belting! We quaked. "Right, for what he has done he is going to get a whacking from this" said Ron. "But before I give it him, who thinks he ought to get two strokes?" Several hand shot up, anxious to see rogue get his just deserts. Unfortunately it was me who was chosen to bend over the bench to receive the suggested number of whacks, which were fortunately given in a light hearted way.

At some time towards the end of the War a concrete framed and brick building was erected at the West End of the school and the Woodwork Shop moved into this for a short period. It later became the Geography Room, presided over by Mr "Sammy" Severn. Then, possibly in 1946, the Education Department took over the ARP building in Albany Road and thus began the expansion of the Handicraft Department at Bemrose School, under the guidance of Mr Hanlon.

Two other members of the Craft Staff I remember were Norman Rogerson, who I believe replaced Mr Pipes when he retired and another small fellow with curly ginger hair. I do not recall his name but at the time there were two characters on radio named "Tish" and "Tosh" and in true schoolboy fashion we applied the names to Mr Hanlon and his colleague. They even joined in the joke and would use catchphrases used by the radio couple.

I do not know if there is still an honours board in the Library, but after the War one was commissioned and this beautiful oak plaque with the names of former pupils killed in the War incised and picked out in blue paint was erected over the fireplace at the East end of the Library. Tragically all the mitred joints at the corners sprang open due to the heat and consequent shrinkage of the timber. The plaque was removed and I last saw pieces of it in the storeroom at Albany Road. I do not know if it was replaced.

In 1950 Woodwork was allowed as a subsidiary subject in the Higher School Certificate Examination for the first time and the four of us duly took the exam. I can remember Ron's consternation when he saw the theory questions and realized that he had not covered one particular aspect of the paper. He quickly consulted the prospectus for the subject and found that it was not listed. He complained to the Examining Board and was able to reassure us that the error would be taken into consideration on marking.

I have always been very appreciative of the education I received at Bemrose School and thankful for the educational opportunities which were available to my generation. Life was not easy and my parents must have made many sacrifices to enable me to take advantage of those opportunities. I shall never forget the only piece of Latin that was important to me. "NON FALLUNT FUTURA MERENTEM" – "the future does not let down he who merits it".

Frank (Noel) Grimshaw and John (J K) Brierley have both published works which give vivid personal recollections of the school during Wartime.

Grimshaw, a prep boy 1937-38, was in the main school from 1939-45, and his book *It was different in my day* reminds us of an age of "ink pots, grey flannel shorts and ration-books". He makes a highly significant point, that any success at school was publicly celebrated. Recognition would be received from the Head himself during School Assembly. It was considered that later in life, competition would inevitably be encountered in all fields, and sooner the rewards of success were personally experienced the better".

He has sharp memories of the local shop, the nearest the school got to a "Tucker" having occasional off-ration biscuits or sweets, of the ignominy of being caned, of going into long trousers with the attendant problem of cycle-clips, and of coasting to and from school in the slip-stream of one of the ubiquitous trolley-buses.

Grimshaw worked in farming before National Service with the Sherwood Foresters; went to an Agricultural College and when a soccer injury "put paid to practical farming" had a successful career as a MAFF advisor in Sussex, North Yorkshire and the Durham Dales.

John Brierley, certainly one of the most literate and articulate of Bemrosians, was at school from 1938-1945, rejoined the school after a brief spell as a newspaper reporter, and left age 18 ½ after Higher School Cert. The army had him for a while, prior to a very successful career in Education which ended with him as a Senior Government Inspector of Schools. Some years ago he published his deeply interesting memoirs, *In the Shadow of the Means Test Man*.

Here you will be reminded of the pride in a new school uniform, the utter bewilderment of your first day or two in the seemingly enormous new building, the complete strangeness of the new regime.

Brierley's book brings into sharp focus the round of school meals, homework and punishments, together with brief bright portraits of some of the staff. He is warmly grateful to the English teachers, Mr House and especially to Miss Higginson.
One man who made a decided imprint on him was D Habib, an Iraqi Gym Instructor whose addition to the staff triggered off a spectacular rise in the number of fractures and other injuries. He taught fencing and this activity peaked in a dramatic duel with sabres between Brierley and Douglas Pimley at Hobbies Day. In retrospect it seems a bit odd that so many diverse and unlikely activities should come under the catch-all of "Hobby".

Fencing practice in School Hall

Chapter 6

E. G. Bennett, 1951-57

(Researched by Peter Grattidge)

In 1951, Eric Geoffrey Bennett MA succeeded Mr MacFarlane as Headmaster. E G Bennett (one suspects that few people knew his Christian names and even fewer addressed him by them) was 40 when he moved from Heckmondwike Grammar School, Yorkshire, where he had been Headmaster from 1948-51.

He was educated at Deacon's School, Peterborough, from 1921-25 and then moved to the City Boys' School, Leicester, from 1925-29. A student at Downing College, Cambridge from 1929-32, he gained a BA 2nd class honours in modern languages (French and German) and was awarded his MA in 1936.

Mr Bennett was not entirely a stranger to Derby when he arrived at Bemrose School as his first teaching post after leaving Cambridge University in 1932 was as Assistant Languages Master at Derby School for two years before moving to the King Edward V1 School, Nuneaton. He joined the army in 1940 and served with the Intelligence Corps in Italy and Austria. He was mentioned in despatches for his services in Italy and was demobilised in 1946 with the rank of Major. For two years, he was Assistant Education Officer with the West Sussex County Council before taking up his post at Heckmondwike.

Most boys who were at the school when E G Bennett arrived were very soon aware of the contrast with his predecessor. Clive Milner, who was later to become a Major-General in the Canadian Army and an Assistant Secretary General at the United Nations, recalled that *"Mr Bennett was, to most of us, an aloof disciplinarian with no sense of humour and a liking for the cane. I was on the receiving end of 10 of his best and had to remain standing the rest of the day!"* Another former pupil summed up the impression of many with his description of the new Headmaster as *"steely-eyed with a withering look from 50 paces that was enough to curb any rebellious thoughts!"* But perhaps these impressions were more vividly held by those boys who had experienced the transition from the avuncular MacFarlane to the disciplinarian Bennett – the pupils starting after Mr Bennett's arrival no doubt accepted his rule as strict but perfectly normal.

The new Headmaster was determined to maintain or raise standards in every aspect of school life. As far as school leaving examinations were concerned, it proved difficult to make comparisons with earlier periods as the new General Certificate Examination (GCE) to replace the earlier School Certificate was introduced at about the same time as Mr Bennett arrived.

The VIth form (Upper and Lower years) comprised about one tenth of the school population. In 1955, the Headmaster reported that there were 40 boys in the VIth form on the Arts side and 35 doing Science (although four of the five boys winning State Scholarships that year were on the science side). The lower number studying Science in the VIth he attributed to the fact that there were many more opportunities to enter an engineering or scientific career at 16. However, the following year he was able to report a marked swing towards science. Of the 36 boys entering the Lower Sixth, twice as many were taking Science course compared to Arts.

Each year, a handful of pupils won University, State, County or other Scholarships and successive Speech Days paid tribute to their achievement. Those gaining University awards in this period included:

1951 J M Innes – Open Scholarship in English at Queen Mary College, London

1952 R H Varney – Open Scholarship in Classics at King's College, London

1953 M J Pickering – Open Scholarship at University College, Oxford

1954 R F Fox and A R Brown – Open Exhibitions at Cambridge

1956 D A Bayliss – Open Exhibition in History at Balliol College, Oxford

Other boys who were singled out for special mention in the annual Speech Day reports on account of their academic achievements included:

B Crowther - second place in all England in the Civil Service Executive Grade examination;

F M Larkin – passed in four A-level subjects – three of them with distinction - "though barely 17 years old"

E A French – sixth in all England in the Civil Service Executive Examination although not qualifying for a Grammar School place until age 13

P Boardman – another pupil entering school at age 13, passed 'A' level in four subjects, was awarded a British Petroleum Scholarship and a County Exhibition

R E Allsop passed all eight of his 'O' level subjects *"with the quite astonishing average of 88%"*

C A F Johnson was the first recipient of the MacFarlane award for classics (endowed by the Old Boys' Association)

B M Smallwood was awarded the Bemrose prize having secured the highest marks in the A level examinations *'at the comparatively young age of 17 years 3 months'*

Academic distinction was by no means confined to examination successes. In 1953, the school won a 'Top of the Form' competition organized by the local authority and the following year the school took part in the national BBC competition. The team of S A Tate, D A Bayliss, J V Tilley and A Godward reached the final of the English schools when they were narrowly beaten by Bournemouth Girls' School.

"Top of the Form", recorded for BBC Radio at Bemrose School in 1954
(L to R) D A Bayliss, John V Tilley, Stephen Tate, Alan Godward.
Photo courtesy Derby Evening Telegraph

In his 1955 Speech Day report, the Head cited television as a possible hindrance to academic achievement. *He had, he said, made enquiries of one of the Vth forms and found "That half the form had television sets at home and were spending on an average 1½ hours every evening watching."* He conceded that *"some of the programmes may well have an educational value"* but *"nevertheless, television is a supine affair."*

Similarly, participation in out of school activities (i.e. the clubs, societies, sports and other activities provided by the school) was limited to some extent because of "the large number of boys who take up part-time, paid employment outside school hours." He acknowledged that *"boys, like the rest of us, could always do with some more money, I suppose"* but he urged parents to question whether such activity was in the boys' best interests.

Music and Drama

The well established tradition of music and drama activities at the school continued to flourish during the Bennett era. On the music side, this was very much due to the seemingly tireless efforts of Mr Kenneth Eade. Mr Eade joined the staff at Bemrose in 1948 and stayed for 9 years. On his leaving the school in 1957, the school magazine recorded *"We owe a great deal to Mr Eade, for he made music one of the most important activities of the school: the choir, the music in the daily service, incidental music of all kinds, the carol concerts, and the operettas in the summer term will remain in our memory. Nothing was too difficult for him to undertake and everything he did was a triumphant success. The most modest of men, he had the gift of inspiring others and the tradition he established will no doubt continue".*

1950 – School Choir and Mr Eade

Mr Eade was largely responsible for the acquisition of the new organ at the school. In 1951, a committee charged with the task of finding and financing an organ authorised Mr Eade to look out for a suitable instrument and in June of that year he visited Chichester High School for Girls which had offered a three-manual organ for sale. He was accompanied by Mr Harris of the Harris Organ Company. They went by car and as a result of a breakdown near Guilford they found themselves stranded for the night but spent the time profitably planning a new specification for the organ which, though suitable, was badly in need of an overhaul. This overhaul was undertaken during the summer and the organ assembled in the gallery of the School Hall during the Autumn.

A Concert and Operetta were performed by the School in July to raise money for the Organ Fund. G J Price played Captain MacGregor in *Once aboard the lugger* and M G Elston was the mate. The bosun was played by D J Hunt with B O Cantrill as Tom the cabin boy. M S Knowles had

the part of Sludgy Meagles (alias Misery a sailor) and other solo parts were taken by P W Shaw, J F Raynes and N C Horton.

At the inauguration in November, Mr John Carter, the Deputy Head and Chairman of the Organ Fund Committee, reported that £550 had been raised, mainly through the Parents' Association, and the Committee looked to the Old Boys to raise the remaining £420 needed. An Organ Recital was given at the inauguration ceremony by Dr William McKie, the organist of Westminster Abbey and the school choir sang *Flocks in pastures green abiding* by Bach and *The strain upraise of joy and praise* specially composed for the occasion by Mr Eade. A brass plate attached to the organ quoted J S Bach *To the glory of God and that my neighbour may benefit thereby.*

On occasions, Mrs Eade combined her talents with her husband's. For the 1956 School Concert Mr Eade set music from Mozart's *Il Seraglio* to an adaptation by Mrs Eade of Hans Anderson's *The Emperor's new clothes.* The result was reported as '*a triumphant success; the choir sang magnificently, the principals (R D Fletcher, W L Wilson and C E Wilne) were excellent in both voice and action, there was some good miming by R D Wilson and R J Pearson… and the final chorus with the organ and the BBB giving full support can only be described as terrific.*'

As well as teaching music throughout the School, Mr Eade also trained the school choir (which was often accompanied by Mr J L Trippett who taught French and Spanish). The choir was repeatedly successful at the Derby and Derbyshire Music Festivals. In July 1952, the choir recorded songs for the BBC Midland Home Service which were broadcast in Children's Hour on 8th January 1953.

Mr Eade also set to music the School Song which had been written by Mr S F Downing a former English Teacher at the School. The song was sung for the first time at the School Speech Day on February 25th 1953:

> *Ours is a hillset city, seen afar;*
> *And ours the unbushelled light, the unshaken star*
> *Above the storm, the lance in swift career*
> *Against the dragon of night-foundered fear.*
>
> *We are the city's sentries, this the hour*
> *Wherein we stand to guard the beacon tower.*
> *The lamp was trimmed and burning when we came;*
> *We pledge to leave as quick and clean a flame.*
>
> *Though others built the tower and shaped the lance,*
> *We have our chapter in the high romance,*
> *With ancient promise that who keeps the sword*
> *In honour, shall not lack the knight's reward.*
>
> *Dawn trumpets rout the shadows: east to west*
> *Illumined lies the country of the Quest.*
> *May we in mettled manhood bear afield*
> *The badge of Bemrose on a blameless shield.*

Drama, especially in the form of the Annual School Plays was largely produced by two members of the English staff; Mr Gordon Hemmings and Miss Olwen Jones. Several productions involved collaboration between Mr Eade and Mr Hemmings. On one occasion, Mr Eade unearthed some tunes from an eighteenth century comic opera by Samuel Arnold and Mr Hemmings wrote entirely new words to fit. The result was *School and Crossbones* performed by the School in July 1953. The lead part (Dame Charlotte Crammer, Headmistress of Parklands Academy) was played by A Wenman and way down the cast list was Joseph Seeds played by M S Knowles. Later that year, Michael Knowles played the lead in *Richard II* giving a *'distinguished performance'*.

In 1954, Michael Knowles, as Henry V *"carried the play on his shoulders ... dominating every scene in which he appeared; his was a fine performance, a fitting climax to a very successful career in school drama."* In his Speech Day report, the Headmaster acknowledged *"In M S Knowles we had an outstanding actor whose successes were equalled by his modesty."* Michael went on, of course, to pursue a very successful acting career. On television he took the parts of Captain Ashwood in *It Ain't Half Hot Mum* and Teddy Meldrum in *You Rang M'Lord?* As well as being an actor Michael is also a prolific writer, for both stage and screen. That 1954 performance of Henry V was remarkable quite apart from any distinguished acting; just before the play, the School was hit by a 'flu virus and 15 of the cast were away from school on the day following the last performance.

1953 production of Richard II featured Michael Knowles, who later went on to RADA and TV fame in classic sit-coms.

If, during his time at School, Michael Knowles was the star performer, there were other stalwarts who rose to the demands of an annual Shakespeare play: D G Allen, M J Allen, R E Allsop, I J Arnot, E G Aspley, D A Bayliss, R M Bonsall, J P Carr, K

E Dove, J Hampton, J Hunt, G H Hunter, M J Pritchard, H Rose, S A Tate, B Thomson, B C Uff amongst others who appeared repeatedly in the cast list.

In addition to the Annual Shakespeare Play, many other boys took part in the annual Plays Festival which involved performances from each School Year. Plays in Latin, French and Spanish as well as English were included. Possibly those participating were not always 'volunteers'. The reviewer of the 1953 production commented on the *"Middle School Revue in which nearly everybody in Forms 3 and 4 seemed to be doing something – a stupendous effort on the part of Miss Jones."*

Behind the scenes, much of the stage management work was done by Mr J A Carter and his helpers. The Art master, Mr I Watts was usually responsible for the scenery.

Sport
Mr Rees and Mr C Loeber were principally in charge of games and sports at this time. The School with the advantage of some 700 boys and extensive Playing Field usually acquitted themselves well against local school opposition. However, the enviable sports facilities did not deter the new Headmaster in his first Speech Day report from lamenting the absence of a second Gymnasium and a Cricket Pavilion.

Bemrose Grammar School 1953-54

Back row (left to right): D.Allen, M.Twelvetrees, P.Foster, R.Bullivant, J.Stanley, E.Noon, T.Walden. Middle row: ?.Wilson, M.Byett, P.Newbery, J.Blakely, D.Dodgson. Front row: R.Shaw, S.Hopkins.

Football was the most popular team game and the School regularly provided several members of the Derby Boys' team. In the 1952-53 season Newbery, Taylor, Smallwood, Jeffrey, Hopkins and Byett were regular members of the Derby Boys' Eleven. Newbery also played in every match for the Derbyshire Boys' side which won the championship for the Midland Counties area that season. Peter Newbery signed professional terms with Derby County after leaving school. In the previous season, the School were undefeated in the Senior League Division 1 and went on to win the Derby County Trophy Competition for Secondary Schools in the County. Antill, Stanley, Fletcher and Twigg were singled out for particular praise. In 1955-56, Jackson played in all the representative matches for the Derbyshire Grammar Schools XI and Blakely captained their B team.

Cricket was the summer sport and although competitive games were played against other schools, one of the most popular fixtures was the Annual School v Staff match. A competitive spirit not only surrounded the playing of this match but also its reporting. In the 1951 game, Adams took two staff wickets for no runs and the scorers consequently reported his average as 'infinity'. Mr Critchlow, however, insisted that there must be some mistake as Adams could only *tend towards infinity* and never really get there!

The School beat the Staff in that match, as they usually did, but the 1955 meeting resulted in a rare tie, both sides scoring 109 runs. Inevitably, team members changed almost annually as boys moved through the School but in the mid-1950's, Aspley, Blakely, Ferneyhough, Galloway, Hewitt, Hodgetts, Holmes, Kent, Mart, Mortlake, Newbery, Tate, Williamson and Wragg were amongst the regular players.

Lacking their own courts (at that time), the School had to use the Rowditch Recreation ground for tennis. The School Team was generally successful although they suffered a 9-0 defeat by Nottingham High School in 1952. However, in the same season they reported a victory by the same score in 'an enjoyable match' against the girls of Parkfield Cedars! Parker, Fox, Woodall, Durrell, Buckland and Heath were regular members of the School Team in that season. Fox and Woodall later being selected for Derbyshire Colts.

Tennis Team with Headmaster E G Bennett and Sports Teacher Danny Rees

The School generally did well in the annual Derby

Secondary School Sports held at the Municipal Sports Ground and often represented Derby in the County Athletic Sports. In the 1952 event, Methven and Haviland established new records in the long jump and Hubball in the hurdles and Kershaw in the 440 yards achieved national standards. All four later represented Derbyshire in the All-England Sports and N L Haviland won the National Long Jump.

In cross-country running, one outstanding runner was A R Selby. In 1954-55, he was first (and I P Francis second) in ten of the thirteen Inter-school Cross-Country Matches. Selby broke the School Record for the course and then broke his own record twice subsequently in that year and Francis broke the School Record for the mile. In later years, Selby lowered the School Record further and in 1957 with Millward and W Wilson he represented Derbyshire in the All-England Championships.

Basketball flourished and became increasingly popular during these years. An annual Inter-house Swimming Gala was always keenly contested.

Gym Display

Library

Some 20 years before this era, when the present School was built, it was Mr A House who ensured that the School had a Library on a scale then far ahead of its time but throughout Mr Bennett's headship, Mr W A Pickering had charge of its organisation and management. In his annual reports, Mr Pickering paid tribute to a number of boys who assisted in various ways and particularly by compiling statistics of library usage. In 1953, tribute was made *"to the apparently inexhaustible enthusiasm and industry of Allsop and his assistants, Eames, Dove, Hewitt and Court in 2L and no less to the painstaking toil of Fowkes in 2M…"* The same team, the following year, was able to analyse the 6,432 book issues over the 23 forms which made up years

one to five (other arrangements applied in the sixth form). The first year boys took out significantly more books than those in any older year and the highest individual score that year was that of Trippett who borrowed a total of 94 books. (The following year, O'Hara took out 120 books in the school year). The statistics were suffic-iently

detailed to reveal not only that November 23rd was the busiest day in that year but also that two first year boys did not borrow any books at all!

Captain W E Johns, Arthur Ransome and G K Evans were the most popular authors at that time and *"Kon Tiki"* was the most borrowed non-fiction work.

Clubs and Societies

The various clubs and societies which existed at the time seemed designed to provide further educational activities in a relaxed and informal atmosphere. Most clubs were run by the boys themselves, mostly Sixth-formers, but often with Members of Staff providing encouragement and support. Changing times and fashions, to say nothing of an annually changing clientele, meant that clubs and societies evolved year on year.

In 1951, a mock election was held under the auspices of the Literary and Debating Society. The result was reported to closely parallel the General Election in a victory for the Conservative candidate, Mitchell, beating Labour, Mullarky, into second place whilst the Liberal, Thomson, lost his deposit. Two years later, the Society abandoned the literary element in favour of debating and considered amongst other topics the need for merging Bemrose with Parkfield Cedars. In 1956, the Debating Society changed its constitution and elected a new committee; I J Arnot, D Bateman, K L Bayliss, G J Harrison, R J Hewitt, D J Hunt, A R Selby, J V Tilley, and B C Uff (who was President). At one debate that year, two Members of Staff, Mr A House and Mr E V Harper, spoke on the motion that *"A Grammar School education destroys initiative"*. Mr Hanlon, in charge of Woodwork at the School, made a gavel and block for the Society's use.

The clubs usually reflected or complemented school curriculum subjects. Chemical, Physics and Biological Societies existed at various times but in keeping with the tendency to change according to current demand and enthusiasm they were merged into a Scientific Society in 1954 and for several years the Society enjoyed well-attended meetings which were addressed at various times by members of staff, visiting speakers and pupils. The boys tackled an impressive array of subjects. In its inaugural year, the society heard talks on 'Electronic digital computers' by L W Litting, 'Gold' by B C Uff, 'The peaceful uses of atomic energy' by J W Hallam and 'Cathode ray tubes' by M G Henstock. The following year, K L Bayliss gave a talk on 'Modern trends in motor car design', D J Hunt spoke on 'Basic radio reception', B L Radford described the construction of a converter for a television set in order to receive commercial programmes and P M Boardman spoke on 'Oil extraction and refining'.

Other interests were catered for. The Chess Club which played matches against other schools and in 1956-57 also against the Parents (the school club won 5-3) and against Rolls Royce Apprentices (which resulted in an 8-0 win for the school). The previous year some club members took part in a display against Harry Golombek the British Champion. C C Williams, then the Club Secretary, succeeded in making a draw in one of the Champion's 55 simultaneous games.

The Christian Union in 1955 extended its membership to fourth, fifth and sixth formers (an earlier organisation had restricted itself to sixth form boys only). Mr E V Harper, Mr Cawthorne, and Mr Turner were staff supporters and occasional speakers at the Union at that time.

A Bell Ringing Society introduced several boys to campanology and handbell ringing. In 1955, R J Stretton rang his first peal and J F Murfin and D K Walklate rang their first handbell peals. Several members rang in Staffordshire, Shropshire and Montgomery that year whilst on an Easter holiday trip. The society seems to have been silenced shortly after that.

Another club which flourished for a season was the Rabbit Club. In 1951, P S Hart was able to report that *"as a result of the judicious breeding and sale of rabbits a large profit has been made from which a dividend will be declared at the end of the year"*. Plans were made for a future breeding programme but the club closed down shortly after that. The fate of any remaining rabbits is not known.

School Trips
The 1950s saw an increase in the number and variety of school trips and holidays. Educational day trips (to Stratford, London, local factories etc) were part of the annual School Year and, in addition, usually during the Easter or Summer holidays, longer organised trips were arranged. Mr Maurer and Mr Severn led an annual Geographical Field Trip, often to some Derbyshire village, and the same Teachers, sometimes with other Members of Staff – Messrs Cook and Loeber in 1954, for instance – organised walking holidays. The Yorkshire Dales, the Isle of Arran and North Wales were some of the areas chosen – because the terrain was sufficiently challenging and the overnight hostels suitably primitive according to some recollections. The cost of the week's trip to North Wales in 1954 amounted to £2.10s.0d for each boy.

An annual Land Camp, at Ingham in Lincolnshire from 1952 but previously at Bearley, Warwickshire, was always well attended and involved the boys in potato picking, corn 'stooking' and other harvesting operations.

Mr Sowter organised a visit to Switzerland most years taking a party of boys assisted by two or three other members of staff. The value of these overseas visits was remarked on by the Head when he learned that one boy, on arrival at Calais, was really astonished to find a notice written in French! Shortly after German language lessons were introduced to the school, contact was made with a school in Dülmen, Germany, with a view to encouraging international understanding and friendship. Dr Hans Schober, an English teacher at the German school, came to Derby in 1951 and provided the school with some information about Dülmen and encouraged the idea of an exchange visit by the two schools. From 1952, annual exchange visits were arranged (firstly by Mr A T Clark, later by Mr Smith) for several years. The first visit to Germany, in 1952, involved only four boys and afterwards D Stephen reported in the *Bemrosia* magazine an occasion when attending classes in the Gymnasium with their German counterparts, *"The classes continued as usual, and we were asked to follow the lesson. I found it very interesting to attend a Latin lesson when we read Cæsar, although the dual-translation was rather trying."* Two years later, the party consisted of 20 boys aged from 13 to 18 and a similar number came from Dülmen to stay in Derby. Mr H Cook also arranged an exchange with some Belgian schoolboys at this time.

Staff

At the end of 1951, H E Davis, the School Secretary left. He was replaced by Miss Judith Selby. There were very few female Members of Staff and Miss Selby's presence was particularly noticeable and a convincing message rapidly passed amongst the boys that the previous year she had been crowned Miss Derby in the town's local beauty contest. It was not only the boys' heads that were turned for she was later to marry Mr E V Harper, a History Master at the School. When Mr Harper left the School in 1956 to become Senior History Master at Dagenham County High School, the Head regretted that the move also deprived him of his Secretary. Amongst other non-academic staff at the school were the School Caretaker, Mr Heffer (appointed in 1930 when the school was opened) and the Mr Hollis the Grounds man who diligently prepared the cricket pitches amongst other duties.

Each year, there were some arrivals and departures amongst the school staff. A list of teaching staff is included in an appendix. During this period, some members of staff retired after very lengthy periods of service at the school including its predecessor in Abbey Street. Mr Crowther (History) left in 1952 having been appointed in 1915. He was in charge of the School Cricket for much of his time. The following year, Mr Baxter (Chemistry) left after 33 years. A keen sportsman, he was still able to produce the highest score and best bowling averages in his last match for the Staff X1 against the School in 1951. Miss Smith (English) joined the staff during the First World War and stayed for 37 years. Mr Watts (Art) retired on grounds of ill health in 1956 after 35 years teaching at the school. In 1957, when the Head, Mr Bennett, left the school, he paid tribute to Mr Carter (Physics and Deputy Head), who retired at the same time after 33 years saying that *"no school could have been better served by its Deputy Headmaster; no Headmaster could have asked for a more helpful and hardworking colleague.... Many calls were made on him; none was made in vain. He had a true sense of vocation, an intense love of Bemrose School and a consuming interest in the welfare of the boys at school and their progress in later life... The School owes him a very large debt..."* Both he and Mr Baxter won the Military Cross in the First World War. Mr Spencer (Chemistry) left at the same time having been appointed in 1921. He was Head of Sidney House for many years. Mr W Smellie (Classics) died after a short illness in 1957. He had been a master since 1924 and was very much involved in the Old Boys' Association. Ken Foy recalled that on Anzac Day, Major Smellie, who had fought at Gallipoli in 1915, would don his First World War uniform and take the class through the Campaign with maps, lantern slides and pieces of Allied and enemy equipment.

*Five Masters with 88 years combined service leave in 1957, including William Spencer,
Science Teacher, joined 1921; Deputy Head John Carter, joined 1924; together with
Headmaster E G Bennett, Kenneth Eade (music) and R C Smith (modern languages).
(with acknowledgement to the "Derby Evening Telegraph)*

Other Staff leaving during these years mostly moved on to other teaching posts elsewhere. Those included Mr Thornton (to King's Lynn 1952), Mr W J Thomas (to Dartford 1954), Mr A T Clark (Blackburn 1954), Mr C Loeber (Matlock 1955), Mr F C Lamb (Wolverhampton 1955), Mr W J Pritchard (to Central School, Derby 1956), Mr L J Sutton (Coleshill 1956), Mr R C Y Smith (Wath-on-Dearne 1957). Mrs Hayward left in 1955 because of her daughter's illness. One tragic loss was that of Mr R G Catton who died in March 1955 from injuries he received in a road accident whilst cycling home from school.

Mr E G Bennett who left at the end of the Summer Term 1957 became Headmaster of Bournemouth School. Mr A House, who had been appointed Acting Head, quoted Mr Bennett's summing up of his impressions of the School during his six years there: *"I was very fortunate,"* Mr Bennett said, *"to find, when I came to Derby, a school so well organised, and enjoying the advantages of excellent buildings, equipment and the sympathetic support of the Governors, the Director and his staff. But looking back over the past six years, what I valued most was the loyal support and willing co-operation of the staff, and above all, their united efforts for the School. If I rarely mentioned individuals in my Speech Day reports it was to avoid invidious and unjust distinctions which might have obscured the truth that any successes of the School were the result of team work performed in the spirit which contributed in no small way to the happiness of the School. I count it a privilege,"* he concluded, *"to have been associated with the School for a small part of its history and I wish Bemrose School every possible success in the future."*

Memories

Half a century on, several former pupils have communicated recollections of their time at the School: Sometimes this has been by way of correspondence appearing at various times in the *Derby Evening Telegraph* or to the *Bemrose School Web Site* (www.bemrose.org). Others responded to the appeal by Marilyn Thompson, the former School Librarian for information specifically for this book. In many cases, those recollections have been included in the main text. Others, which may have faded with the passing years or even embellished with fond recall, cover aspects ranging from members of staff to school dinners and the smell of the chemistry labs. Several pupils of the period when the wearing of the School Cap was compulsory recall a ritual burning of those items on the last day of school. Leaving the ashes outside the Head's Study may have been more wishful thinking than reality.

David Hunt (1949-56) recalls forming with several other boys including, amongst others, Geoffrey Lewis, Hedley Hunter and Peter Boardman a 'dating society' to counteract the frustration of being a boys only school. Members, who had to be of a certain age, were sworn to secrecy. They paid one shilling for enrolment and 6d for each introduction. The girls' names were submitted by contacts at Parkfields Cedars, Homelands, Derby High School and Ockbrook School. Financially the scheme was so successful that if a boy was hard up on the night his date fell due, he could have an interest free loan of up to 7s 6d. Strict rules were applied and both girls and boys could be suspended from the scheme if their conduct fell below certain standards. In the case of a boy, being "too fresh with a girl or spending less than 2s 6d on her" were enough to warrant suspension. The scheme proved very popular but unfortunately for the organisers, the national press got wind of the set-up and an article appeared in the *Daily Mirror* (11th July 1955). Confession time followed but not surprisingly the Head seems to have reacted calmly.

Ray Hollis (1953-58) was the son of the School Groundsman so during Ray's time at the School, Mr Hollis Senior, who in his day was no mean cricketer, qualified to play for the Parents' team against the School. As Richard Hann and John Bowers were also at the School then, their fathers, Derby County trainers of the era, were also enlisted.

The 1950s also saw the arrival of 'Rock 'n' Roll' and Tony Ormerod, recalled that although Bemrose was not the sort of institution which tolerated demonstrations of pupil power, those teachers on Dinner Duty one day in 1956 were unable to prevent most of form 5T from giving an impromptu performance of *Heartbreak Hotel* between courses. In lieu of percussion, dessert spoons banged lustily on table tops, only partially drowning out the dreadful din of 20 or so adolescent voices raised in a paean of praise to Elvis. Tony was once reprimanded by the Head after being caught smoking in the Gaumont Cinema and he recalled that R Sluzarenko, a fellow-pupil, was asked by Mr Bennett, *"Do you smoke?"* to which Sluzarenko replied, *"No thank you, Sir, I've just put one out!"*

Mike Creasey (1950-55) recalled almost all of his Teachers and many of their distinguishing characteristics. *"Phyllis Jones standing by the East Gate sending back anyone who had the temerity to use the wrong drive - the left hand one for cyclists, the right hand one for pedestrians; Mr Crowther in his spats walking from the bus stop; Kate Smith collecting her weekly joint from the local butchers', Herbert Cook always seemed to be carrying armfuls of books and Ikey Watts and Bill Pickering with their push bikes."*

Anton Rippon, one of many who recalled their time at Bemrose with fondness and gratitude, quoted a fellow pupil, John Cheadle, who summed up the collective experience: *"Bemrose taught us how to think and how to behave. It gave us the standards that have seen us through life ".*

First XI Cricket Team 1953/4

Intermediate football team, 1951. League Champions and Trophy Winners 1950-51
(Left to right) **Back row:** *A Hutchby, R Jeffery, B Smallwood, Mr A H Sowter, M Taylor, P Newbery, R Dennis.* **Front row:** *M. Byet, K Fryatt, J Green, C Perry, A Dethick*

Sports Day 1953

1954 Jubilee Celebrations

Water colour painting of the school
by art teacher "Ike" Watts 1952

CHAPTER 7

Dr W R C CHAPMAN (1958-71)

A Personal View by Arthur Titterton, 1959 – 1966

Dr. Chapman actually wrote to me (or should I say my parents) before I entered the school. I daresay that he actually wrote the same letter to every pupil, but I gave no thought to that in 1959. I remember there were pages of items that my parents had to buy (most of which they could ill afford). The school uniform, sports equipment, the list seemed endless. It was accompanied by a list of school rules, if anything was ever designed to frighten a new pupil, that list certainly was.

It was with great trepidation that I headed for Bemrose School for the first time in the first week in September 1959. My first sighting of the Headmaster was in our first assembly having lined up dutifully with 800 other boys in the Great Hall, there was I with 30 others in my form 1S staring up at the stage. There were two teachers wearing suits covered by long gowns. There was a hush as Dr Chapman mounted the steps at the side of the stage and proceeded neatly across the stage to centre left. He was a dapper man, a very neat suit, he had a full gown and to my astonishment, a mortar board. Before that, I had only seen that form of dress on Mr Quelch in episodes of Billy Bunter. He stood still and organ music pervaded the Great Hall encouraging some of the 800 gathered to sing or mumble words from an ancient hymn.

I remember vaguely his address and being welcomed to the school, but I spent more time pondering about all those school rules and whether I was ever likely to keep them. That turned out to be my first and last assembly in 7 years at the school. I was of the Catholic persuasion and learned the following day that we Catholics had our own separate assembly and only joined the main assembly for the last few minutes for the Notices. I quite wonder how it is today at the old school with so many ethnic groups and Catholics, whether there is anybody left in a full assembly! At 11 years of age and for the first time experiencing the pomp and ceremony of such a simple matter as a school assembly, I could not help reflecting at that tender age why a Doctor should be in charge of a school! Naivety is a wonderful thing.

Over the next 7 years, apart from an occasional 'Good morning Headmaster' whilst passing in the corridor, the Headmaster never actually spoke to me personally at all. However, he did choose to write to me each term always at the foot of my Report. I still have that Report 39 years on and two of his epistles read, "Although his work is not yet of a satisfactory standard, he has been making a much better effort and deserves praise for it" (8th April 1960) and "I think he is making good progress" (20th July 1962) and finally (before he gave up writing to me in this way) "He must work much harder if he is to achieve anything worthwhile" (17th July 1964). I suppose that is why I became a Solicitor!

It was not until June 1966 whilst in the VIth Form that I had my first (of two) meaningful conversations with Dr. Chapman. For the first time in almost 7 years I entered the Headmaster's Study on the corner of the ground floor on the West Wing. Up to that point I was unaware that he knew that I existed apart from the short epistles on my Report. He, apparently, knew of my wish to go into Law. He had, he told me, through one of his many contacts established there was a position to be offered in a legal firm in town and he invited me to consider making an application for the position. A few days later I had my second and last conversation in that hallowed chamber advising him that I would accept his advice and take up the offer and the result was that after three interviews I gained a position in that Law Firm. Forty years on I have my own firm and have over the years communicated with Headmasters just like Dr. Chapman had done for me, helping others into the legal profession. The circle is therefore complete.

In such a large and elite Grammar School, a pupil would have no conception about the real status of the Headmaster. No real perception as to what he did from day to

day, what his responsibilities were and how he performed them. Pupils today still take their Headmasters for granted and probably always will. It is only with maturity that one comes to realise what a fine leader and figurehead Dr Chapman was, clearly still cherished many years on by all those connected with Bemrose School through his years there both Pupils and Masters.

Dr. Chapman's name was synonymous with Bemrose School. As a Headmaster he knew exactly where Bemrose School was going and he

Dr W R C Chapman PhD (Innsbruck)
Headmaster from 1958 - 1971

steered the School carefully and accurately along that path. One only had to be in assembly on any morning to appreciate the great pride in his voice when announcing that we had beaten this school or that school at some sport and a particular depth of pride when he would announce that a particular Old Boy had gone on to achieve some particular honour or achievement. He vicariously shared in every success the School had, equally he would take personally any criticism levelled at the School or its pupils. He was always very careful to ensure that standards of behaviour were rigorously maintained.

Headmasters and teachers only had surnames. Some had nicknames; Dr Chapman's most common were 'the cheese' or 'cheesy' (doubtless attributed to his ever present smile) and "the beak" to name but two. These, of course, were terms of endearment and not ridicule. A teacher in later life once told me that to have a nickname from the boys was something of a status symbol in the Staff Room!

As pupils we had no idea what a headmaster did other than turn up at assembly most mornings. With maturity we know that he will have attended endless policy meetings, placated the Local Education Authority and supervised, organised and ran a staff of in excess of 75. That, of course, was without considering the pure logistics of 800 boys, an Office Staff, Health and Safety issues and not to mention perhaps the occasional teaching session.

Who can recall the "period system"? There were 40 periods in a week, 8 in a day, 5 in the morning and 3 in the afternoon. Every 40 minutes the bell rang and like musical chairs without the music (and it seemed to me the bell never allowed "travelling time") 800 boys would move around the school from lesson to lesson like a well oiled machine. Did it ever cross anyone's mind how that timetable was achieved?

*Presentation of the Major Smellie M.C., M.A.
Memorial Lectern 1957 by Mr N A Taylor
(Chairman of Old Bemrosians)
Photo courtesy Derby Evening Telegraph*

On good authority from Mrs Mary Bucknall (Dr Chapman's daughter) that it was her father who often had sleepless nights during the summer holidays constructing the timetable with pencil and rubber and bits of coloured card. Can you imagine the five dimensional conundrum, 800 boys, 75 teachers, 40 periods, 15 subjects and thirty class rooms? That matrix was constructed by Dr Chapman every year. Today I suspect it would even give a computer a headache!

None of us boys in those days knew that during the war Dr Chapman had served his country in the RAF as a Flight Lieutenant with RAF Intelligence gaining the honour of being Mentioned in Dispatches in June 1945.

Fluent in German, he spent much of the early part of the war at Bletchley Park in Buckinghamshire, now the legendary centre of the allies crucial efforts to crack the German Enigma code. It was his job to try and make sense of the garbled German which resulted from the efforts of other fine intellectual brains around him trying to unscramble details revealed via the Enigma code machine. From Bletchley Park he was posted to Egypt in advance of the Battle of El Alamein. He was in command of a listening post – sending back all manner of intelligence to Bletchley Park. As the Allies advanced he moved with the advance and saw continued service in Italy where he was "Mentioned in Dispatches". With his usual un-assumed modesty, he once said, "I was never told what it was for, but I suspect it was for discovering a flight of German reconnaissance aircraft which were based at Bihac in the former Yugoslavia. It was after I reported their existence that America flying fortresses wiped them out". He spent the last year of the war back at Bletchley Park using his unique skills to advance the war effort. It was not until 1975, some 30 years after

GO FORTH INTO THE WORLD IN PEACE;

BE OF GOOD COURAGE; HOLD FAST TO THAT WHICH IS GOOD;

RENDER TO NO MAN EVIL FOR EVIL; STRENGTHEN THE FAINT-HEARTED;

SUPPORT THE WEAK; HELP THE AFFLICTED; HONOUR ALL MEN.

WHATSOEVER THINGS ARE TRUE, WHATSOEVER THINGS ARE HONEST,

WHATSOEVER THINGS ARE JUST, WHATSOEVER THINGS ARE PURE,

WHATSOEVER THINGS ARE LOVELY, WHATSOEVER THINGS ARE OF GOOD REPORT;

IF THERE BE ANY VIRTUE, AND IF THERE BE ANY PRAISE,

THINK ON THESE THINGS.

The Prayer
used by Dr Chapman at the final Assembly every year

the war ended, that he was allowed to speak publicly for the first time about what he had done. Even then the Official Secrets Act meant that he could only be factual about involvement rather than detailed. He once said when interviewed and referring to the German surrender on May 8th 1945: "Working in intelligence we knew it was about to occur so I managed to get a few days leave in advance and spent VE Day with my wife and son in Manchester". With that dry wit and unassuming modesty that he was renowned for, he went on to say, "We spent it very quietly. I assumed my role in the war was over, you see".

Even in his eighties when pressed about his war time activities, he would be characteristically modest and say that they were "very un-heroic". He explained that even his wife did not know what he did. His cover story was that he was working for the Foreign Office, although he felt some people thought he might be a spy because he could speak fluent German. Dr Chapman had trained as an RAF Wireless Operator and once said that he would have been happy spending the war in total obscurity. He said that he did not volunteer his knowledge of German at first because he did not fancy being shot behind enemy lines as a spy. It is quite clear even on the little knowledge that is available even so many years after the end of the war that Raymond Chapman probably played more of a part in defeating the enemy that he will ever be given credit for publicly. It was rumoured that prior to his death in 1998 that he had prepared a book about his life in the Services and in particular at Bletchley Park. It was, I believe, to be published posthumously, but nothing has so far appeared.

Dr Walter Raymond Carson Chapman was a Yorkshire man born in Bradford. He was educated at Hanson School and then Sheffield University where he obtained First Class Honours in English in 1932. In 1933 he took his MA Degree and Diploma in Teaching. From 1933 – 34 he was in Innsbruck University gaining a PhD in English and German. From 1935 – 1945, excluding his war service, he was a Master in North Manchester Grammar School teaching English and German. From 1946 to 1948 he was Senior English Master at Queen Elizabeth Grammar School, Blackburn and moved on to be Headmaster of Firth Park Grammar School in Sheffield where he remained as Headmaster until 1957.

He became a Derbian on his appointment to the Headship of Bemrose Grammar School from the 1st January 1958 and he there steered that particular ship in a successful style until his retirement on the 31st December 1971. He was only 48 years of age and to be in charge of perhaps the most elite Grammar School in the whole of Derbyshire demonstrates how well thought of he was among his peers and certainly what a splendid choice it was by the then Governors.

He made Derby his home; he brought his family up in Derby, his two boys and a girl and remained a Derbian until his death on the 16th September 1998.

Official opening of the Tennis Courts

In 1966 Dr Chapman was appointed a Magistrate to the Derby Bench and there served dutifully for 14 years. He was also a Warden at Derby Cathedral, the Chairman of Derby Council of Churches and an active member of Derby Rotary Club. Such was Raymond Chapman's contribution to his adopted town that in the millennium year he was nominated as one of the City's outstanding achievers of the millennium. He was nominated by fellow Rotarian Dermot Murray of Quarndon who said of him, "I felt absolutely compelled to nominate Dr Chapman. The first thing that struck me about him was his intelligence and the more I found out about him the more I respected him which I am sure many people do. His major influence in the City was as an educator and the dedication and kindness he showed his pupils at Bemrose is remembered by a great many people".

Although I left Bemrose School in 1966 and became a modestly successful Solicitor, I never had the privilege of appearing before Dr Chapman on the local Bench, but I did meet him in 1994 when he and I were both involved in different ways in supporting the development of the new Derby Independent Grammar School. I remember chatting to him one day and reminding him what he had said about me in Reports and with his usual wit and erudition he said "It only proves that I was right, if you work hard you will achieve". That, of course, was something I had learned long ago, but it was very pleasing to have such an endorsement from the great man himself.

I am sure, like myself, there will be hundreds of old Bemrosians who perhaps never had any real contact with Dr Chapman whilst at school, but will always be aware of what a superb job he did in captaining the ship that was Bemrose School from 1958 through to 1971. Once when interviewed he said "My philosophy was simple – to ensure every boy achieved his potential whatever his ability. I thought it (Bemrose) was an excellent school. It had a good environment and a delightful Library and the boys looked smart and were courteous and I was fortunate that I had some excellent colleagues." With typical self deprecation he went on to say "At times I thought I was being paid a great deal of money for not doing much work."

Until June 1966 I thought that I was unknown to Dr W R C Chapman, but I was wrong and I suspect he has proved many boys wrong both before and after that. He set me carefully on the first step of my career ladder and for that I thank him dearly.

When he decided to retire in 1971 it marked the end of an era both for Bemrose Grammar School and Dr Chapman. Although he could have gone on teaching and being Headmaster for a further four years, he decided that it was a watershed and as Comprehensive Education was due to come in the following year, he said "I was being asked to make a number of policy decisions, but it seemed honest and honourable to go so my successor would not be bound by the decisions I had made". That honesty and integrity was his trademark. Concerning retirement it was written about him that "When it comes to growing old gracefully, he could hold a Master Class". When a local reporter asked him what he was going to do in retirement he replied "I seek to bring a touch of class and a dash of honour to what Adam Smith called the natural indolence of old age." He enjoyed retirement from paid employment for 17 years, but he was far from indolent in that period spending many hours on Committees giving of his time and experience freely, one of the many beneficiaries being the formation of the Derby Independent Grammar School.

It was with sadness to pupils and friends and family alike that his death on the 16th September 1998 was announced. He was 88 years of age. His close friend for many years, Dr Michael Levaux spoke at his request at his Funeral. Dr Levaux described him "As a beacon of wisdom, courtesy and good sense ...." "Although a gentle man, he was capable of carrying out a stern authority when it was necessary. Under his hand Bemrose went from strength to strength, Bemrose boys emerged to go to Universities, join a profession and gain Honours".

Dr Raymond Chapman would be the first to acknowledge that he was simply the Captain of an excellent ship. It had an excellent crew, but it had to be led and it was led with authority, good grace and honour and integrity. I doubt there are many former pupils who had the privilege of attending between 1958 and 1971 who would disavow that premise. The school motto on every VIth Form blazer badge was "Non Fallunt Futura Merentem" which translated means "The future does not let down those who merit it". That, I think, is what he meant when he wrote on my Report in 1964 "He must work much harder if he is to achieve anything worth while". He knew that was right then, it has taken me the better part of 40 years to appreciate it.

Raymond Chapman was a figure of consistency in a changing world and a model of dignity and honour and it is unlikely we will see his kind again.

SCHOOL STAFF 1963

Back Row *John Mallon (Lab Assistant), (?2), Harry "Pobble" Calvert, K Capp, Peter Bateman, "Thicky" Goodwin, Mr Heffer (Caretaker) Albert Pipes, Arthur Marsh (Lab Assistant), Ronnie Hanlon.* **Third Row** *Jim Tate (Chemistry), Dave Amedro, John Sutton, Mr E "Taffy" Davies, Bill Barnett, Mr Dorrell, Jack Mathers, Danny Rees, Ken Piercy, Nigel Savigny, Arthur Pope.* **Second Row** *Mildred King (Secretary), Brenda ? (Secretary), (?3), W Nunn, Bill Gray, Charles Kitchell (RE), Narry Holt, Bill Grimadell, Keith Hand, Malc Warwick, Dave Williamson, Mrs Bonehill (Canteen Manager).* **Front Row** *Mr P Maurer, Bill Pickering, Herbert Cooke, J R Molyneaux, "Piggy" Sowter, William Norville, W R C Chapman (Headmaster) aka "Cheese", Alan Goddard, Sammy Severn (Geography), ?Fred Palmer (Chemistry), Jake Harbach (Physics), Dicky Marriot, Polly Hepworth.*

BEMROSE TEACHING STAFF c1963

AMEDRO, David 'Pedro', English, Spanish and French from 1959

ARNOTT, Ian J, English 1964-69

BARNETT, William Tom, Geography 1945-71, Head of Economics

BATEMAN, Peter 'Flap'

BRANTHWAITE, Eric William, English 1945-64

BROWN, J N, Modern Languages 1960-63

CALVERT, nickname 'Pobble', Mathematics from 1960

CAPPS, K A, Science 1960-63

CARSON, called 'Mad', Jack from 1969

CHAPMAN, Dr W R C, Headmaster 1958-71

CHANDLER, Rev J E O, Head of RE from 1965

COOIL, Arthur L, Mathematics 1928-45 then returned in 1958 for 4 more years

COOK, Herbert, Head of Modern Languages from 1948

CUNNINGHAM, M B, Russian from 1970

DAVIES, A, English 1958-63

DORRELL, Colin David, German and French from 1957

FORDHAM, A, Head of History 1969-71

FORREST, M St J, Classics, 1964

GATLAND, Paul G. 'Tiny', History, English and General Studies 1964-69

GIBBS, G L, pupil and then became English teacher in 1966

GODDARD, A, 1949

GOODWIN, C W, 1962

GRAHAM, D, History 1960-63

GRAY, W J, 1962

GRIMADELL, C W, Physics from 1952

HAND, E R, Art Teacher 1956

HANLON, Ronald Francis, pupil in 1929 then taught Handicrafts 1940-78

HARBACH, Jake 'Harry', Head of Physics 1931-78

HAWLEY, Science from 1964

HEATH, R J, Biology/Chemistry, from 1964

HINDLEY, S, Head of English 1967

HOLT, D N, Physics from 1960-65

JOHNSON former pupil who joined the staff to teach Music, 1967

KITCHELL, Charles J, taught Theology and coached Games from 1958

LOCH, P E, left 1963

MANCHESTER, L, Physics from 1958-61

MARRIOTT, Richard

MATHERS, C John 'Jack', Mathematics 1946-72

MAURER, Paul E 'Monkey', Geography 1947-71

MOLYNEAUX, J Roger, French and Maths 1942-71

NADEN, John 'Noddy' was first a pupil and then taught Physics

NORVILL, W C 'Nunkie', History 1930-65

NUNN, G R, Mathematics and Physics from 1957-64

ORCHARD, History from 1960

PALMER, Fred, Chemistry 1955-71

PICKERING, William Archie 'Percy', English 1935-73

PIERCY, E B, Biology from 1960

PIPES, Arthur Haynes, Woodwork 1947-67

POPE, Dr Arthur, Music 1958-65

REES, Danny E B, P.E. teacher from 1950

ROTHWELL, Norman J 'Big Louie', History and Deputy Head

SEVERN, Maurice 'Sammy', Geography 1946-72

SHAW, P A, former pupil joined the staff teaching Maths, 1964

SMITH, Duncan Charles, taught History and Government from 1969

SOWTER, Arthur 'Piggy', French and German 1948-72

SUTTON, John S, Head of History, 1960-68

TATE, Jim M, a pupil from 1944-52, taught Chemistry 1958-71

TAYLOR, A, 1965-70

TRIPPETT, John Leslie, taught French and Spanish from 1943-59

UNDERWOOD, J A, was teacher of Chemistry and Biology 1964-71

WARWICK, Malcolm A, taught Russian 1958-65

WELLS, S E H, Head of English 1964-67

WHEATLEY, 'Stu' J, taught Science

WILLETTS, J H 'Ben', Classics 1967-71

WILLIAMSON, David, 1962-67

NEWTON HOUSE PREFECTS AND MONITORS
1958 - 59

BACK ROW (L. to R.)
1) McDowell 2) Hatch 3) J.M. Naden* 4) R.M. Warner 5) Hiles*
6) C. Oldam* 7) D. Hemsley 8) Crick 9) Maunder 10) Margetts.
11) K. Stapleford.

Front Row
1) Wragg 2) H. Norvill* 3) R. Wilson* (school capt) 4) D. Petts*
(House Capt.) 5) Dr. W.R.C. Chapman M.A. (Headmaster)
(6) Mr. Molyneaux (House Master) 7) A. Williams* (House
Vice-Capt.) 8) Slack* 9) Blockley 10) P.C. Clarke.

* Prefects
Rest Monitors.

Brian Waters - in the Late Developers Stream

I was one of 27 boys, gathered from Secondary Schools across Derby who became the 1966 "T" stream at Bemrose Grammar School. This was effectively a "13 +" class, formed from boys transferred from other Secondary Schools to Bemrose on the recommendation of their Headmaster. This very selective late entry meant that to enjoy success at GCE "O" level after only three years demanded much, not only in terms of ability, but also in commitment to learning at a time in life when the transition from boy to man interfered in every way possible. Whilst some scholars were successful in a spectacular fashion and some failed miserably, most were just average. Spanish, generally accepted to be the easiest to learn, was the only foreign language taken because of the reduced time scale. The success of this late transfer was to a very large degree dependent on the individual, tempered by effective teaching of the group of "late developers".

The very first time I met the Headmaster Dr Chapman was at the interview during which he would decide whether or not he would agree to me transferring from Littleover Secondary Modern School. The interview lasted well over an hour, although it seemed to fly by for me. I remember sitting in front of his desk, a desk that seemed to swallow him up. Dr Chapman was not a big man, but he had presence. He put me at my ease from the commencement of the interview and asked me a great many questions - How much did I read? How often did I read? What did I read? Did I read the newspapers? He asked me about the political situation at the time, the arts, the sciences and what did I want to do when I left school. I cannot remember individual answers but what I did say must have pleased him because I was invited to join the T-stream.

My very first day as a third year pupil at Bemrose School, September 5th 1966, dawned bright and clear. By 9am I had walked the mile or so to school and was lined up in the school playground with 26 other boys, all dressed in very new uniforms and all acutely aware of the scrutiny of other boys from inside the building. I was pleased to see two boys in this new class were old acquaintances from Junior School. Within a few minutes a roll call had been briskly taken, we formed up into a single line and were led inside. Our base classroom was located on the first floor. For the rest of that academic year, we would be known as "3T". Our form Master was Mr "Pop" Goddard he would be in charge of us in an administrative sense throughout our school lives and we would be based in the same classroom throughout that time.

Each boy was assigned to a "House", the intention being to encourage competition. At every level within the School, both physical and academic, there were opportunities to gain points for one's house. I was allocated to Newton House, the House Master was Mr "Ning" Molyneux, an amiable fellow with white hair, unfortunately given to complex facial twitching. The entire complement of house members would congregate at "House Meetings". The attention of many of the boys would be on Mr Molyneux, not for his announcements but looking for variations on his twitch which could be perfected for the delight of chums later.

Every pupil had a desk. The single desks at Bemrose were wooden, with hinged "lids" and inkwells, ball pens had not been invented! Each desk lid could tell a story for the occupants over many years. The contents of desks, and the storage strategy employed, often gave valuable clues to the habits of the desk's owner. Some desks were used for minimal storage while others would be so full that the lids did not shut properly. Most desks would be untidy, although occasionally there would be desks set out and maintained to very high standards. End of term desk housekeeping was an activity undertaken by all.

In common with many other schools, we were required to wear school uniform. The Bemrose uniform was often the second outfit to have been purchased at quite considerable expense within a two year period. Uniform consisted of a maroon blazer, shirt with school tie and grey trousers. School caps were still being worn then but were an "optional extra". Other items included P.E. and sports kit, white apron for handicrafts, satchels, colloquially referred to as "sacks", for books and kit, sometimes replaced by the odd brief case.

The first day sped by in a blur. Whilst most of the Masters were generally very patient and helpful on that first day, others were not so charitable, a few making it clear that they considered new boys in the third year a pestilence. Everything was so new and so different. After the narrow corridors and low ceilings of my previous school, the high ceilings and "glass walls" gave the buildings a spacious feel which was a welcome change. The polished wooden parquet flooring of the corridors and classrooms attenuated the noise of the tramping of many pairs of feet. Irrespective of the volume of traffic along the corridors, there were rarely any "person jams".

Discipline

Without discipline, personal work suffered, and it was important to have order and a means of enforcement, for without it there would have been chaos, not just in the judicial sense. Equally, it was important that personal discipline was cultivated because on warm summer evenings when the outdoors and friends beckoned, it took quite a bit of discipline to resist the temptation and get on with homework. Of course, on many occasions the temptation became too strong, but that's another story!

School discipline was a very easy system to understand in so far as you did as you were told, when you were told. On a personal basis the lowest level of "offence" was related to work. Late submission of work, or unacceptably poor work, were common offences likely to be punished by more work or a detention. School detention was relatively serious and could appear on one's report. Offenders usually had to do "sums" for an hour after school. Public order offences such as talking in class or other disruptive behaviour could also bring extra work or detention. "Lines" – repetitive copying – a useless exercise designed to bore the offender into mending his ways.

Outside of the classroom, the scope for inadvisable behaviour widened considerably. Anyone found fighting, for instance, might receive a good telling off for a first offence. A second offence would almost certainly lead to detention.

Offending and getting caught a third time would usually mean a trip up the stairs to the East tower, the lair of Mr Rothwell, the Deputy Headmaster. The ensuing interview might hurt, depending upon the outcome of enquiries. "Big Louie" as he was often referred to, was ideally suited to administer punishment, not because he had a sadistic nature, but because of his bulky, glowering appearance. If Mr Rothwell was judge and jury, then his "policemen" were the Prefects, selected members of the Sixth Form, who were officially invested with powers to apprehend or refer offenders. If the offence was bad enough, the process would be short circuited, and the offender would be on his way to see Mr Rothwell directly. Interestingly, for offences deemed to be sufficiently heinous, the Headmaster was personally involved. Corporal punishment was an accepted part of school life in those days.

Discipline resulted in respect being shown to all adults and prefects; indeed, the passage of the Headmaster along the corridor was generally enough to turn the volume of any chatter down to almost a whisper. We all knew exactly what we could and couldn't do, and knew equally well what would happen if we did.

As a final observation on this subject, my experience of the school system was that it was fair. Where doubt existed, then those accused were given the benefit of it, and punishment was not given unless warranted.

A Typical Day

Every school day began with registration in form classrooms, where surnames would be barked out with machine gun rapidity, the responses, or lack of, were noted, and the register updated accordingly. This procedure was immediately followed by assembly, when the entire school would troop into the hall and stand in line, form by form, all facing the stage. There was a brief service followed by any notices.

At midmorning break the boys were released into the great outdoors. There were open and covered play areas available, so inclement weather did not pose a problem. Free school milk was available, and a stack of crates full of small milk bottles was always standing adjacent to the external door to the playground. Those boys that did not take any milk were always more than made up for by those boys who did, the latter often drinking the contents of several bottles! During the warmer months of the year, school milk could be deliciously cool or nauseatingly warm, depending on the length of time between delivery and consumption. Breaks were nominally supervised and a member of teaching staff would normally be about. If this was not the case and one was needed, for some medical attention for example, then someone would have to go and knock on the Staff Room door for assistance. The instant the door was opened, an overpowering plume of tobacco smoke was emitted that became instantly and chokingly noticeable. Many Masters smoked, no doubt to calm their nerves!

Chess Team April 1967

At lunchtimes, those boys who lived near enough to school went home. Those staying for school dinner would line up ready for admittance to the School Refectory. The food at Bemrose was generally very palatable. Waste was anathema to the catering staff, having spent all morning cooking, so when everyone had finished, the invitation was made for those who wished to have "seconds". I remember I partook of "seconds" and "thirds" on one particular occasion!! My favourite part of the meal was the sweet, especially if it was served with custard. I adored school custard! Unfortunately for me, the recipe remained a closely guarded secret because I have never tasted the like since!

School Orchestra 1961/2

Dr Chapman and the School Prefects 1966

There was no break in the afternoon and at five minutes past four each day the bell would ring signifying the end of school. Boys would erupt out of classrooms and disappear at high speed homewards. Homework was an important part of school life, and we could expect at least two homework subjects each day. The complexity, and thus the completion time, of homework increased as the journey through the academic calendar progressed.

The Staff

Every member of Bemrose teaching staff was an expert in his field. Some Masters were unquestionably highly qualified. Some operated at genius level, some were undoubtedly eccentric and some were able to demonstrate a real empathy with their pupils. Almost without exception, each Master had a nickname, usually based on some singularity of appearance or behaviour or both.

Most masters wore gowns, and depending on the individual, appearances ranged from "Mr Chips" to vampire bats! It was a stirring sight to see a Master travelling at best cruising speed, gown billowing behind. Most Masters' gowns had seen a lot of service and with the passage of years, the accretion of chalk dust and other pollutants had corrupted the base black colour to a nondescript grey. Masters seldom adjusted their gowns and consequently, they would slip down at the back, thus putting the hem of the gown at great risk of damage. Indeed, there were several Masters whose gowns were so ripped, they badly needed replacing. But, even the most dilapidated gown would get a makeover on Speech Day when hoods were brought out of storage and worn, displaying the academic achievements of the wearer. Mortar boards were not worn, although there is evidence that Headmasters did wear them if the occasion was important enough.

Dr Chapman was a normally a quietly spoken man but his voice carried when the occasion demanded. His nickname of "Cheese" probably originated from his almost perpetual smile. He was always immaculately dressed. He was a Magistrate. Under his management, the School offered an impressive range of Foreign Languages that included Russian, French, German, Latin and Spanish. In retrospect this was pioneering work on Dr Chapman's part as the development of the European Community and globalisation generally has put a greater emphasis on the requirement for foreign languages. Bearing in mind that during the time in question Britain had not joined the European Union and Russia was still very firmly a Communist country, this was indeed visionary.

Our Mathematics master was Mr "Pobble" Calvert, a short, bespectacled individual, inclined to rotundity, who had distinctive short curly hair and prominent ears. He always seemed to wear a somewhat disreputable jacket with leather-patched elbows. I shall always remember the first Maths lesson on the first day in September 1966 because I got a "Spangle", a small fruit flavoured boiled sweet, introduced during the 1960s, which he issued as an encouragement. His classroom conversation would often be enlivened with odd phrases and words which I found most amusing, and which, with typical schoolboy enthusiasm, I copied at every opportunity. Unfortunately, the intricacies of Mathematics often eluded me and I would spend endless hours surreptitiously looking out of the window, or watching the clock or both. "Waters!" would come the dreaded challenge and I would stammer my way through a woefully inadequate answer. Occasionally, my answer was correct and a Spangle would come hurtling my way! Mr Calvert was an enthusiastic philatelist and a lifelong cricket fan. Any boy showing an interest in either would be guaranteed an attentive ear and advice and help almost without limit. I had an interest in philately, and Mr Calvert would be prepared to talk about stamps almost indefinitely! A non-motorist, Mr Calvert used the bus daily to travel from his home in Melbourne.

"Grazimunda!" was a favourite exclamation often heard in response to the receipt of a correct answer. What it means is anyone's guess, and searches of dictionaries and the Internet have so far yielded no clues. Another favourite of mine was "Oriental Sneetelbeak"!

English lessons were taken by Mr Gibbs, a young, debonair individual, whose tastes in music in particular, were in tune with those of his pupils. The Beatles were at the pinnacle of their musical careers and their album *Sgt Peppers Lonely Hearts Club Band* provided endless opportunities to listen to tracks and discuss the use of language in the lyrics. We were never quite sure what the initial "L" in his name stood for so we nicknamed him "Lance"! English was divided into the study of language and literature. Whilst standard works such as *Catcher in the Rye* and *Henry IV Part One* formed a sizeable part of our literature study, we also took in-depth looks at other books. *Puckoon* by Spike Milligan and *2001 – A Space Odyssey* by Arthur C. Clark were probably the best received in this category. Whilst these works were, without a doubt meritorious in their own right, they were not mainstream school English Literature, but studying them gave us a chance to debate the use of contemporary language. Indeed, such was the reaction to *Puckoon* that I can say with some accuracy, that even those boys who had not previously shown much interest in English became very enthusiastic towards this element of study! To illustrate, most chapters in the book ended in a similar way – the central character "Milligan" would have a short dialogue with a crow thus: "Caw" said the crow, "Balls" said the Milligan!

To assist in our understanding of *2001*, I recall that we attended the ABC Cinema, which in 1968-69 was in East Street, Derby, to watch the film! Mr Gibbs was not particularly strict, preferring to steer rather than lead. I am grateful to him for showing me the ways in which language not only conveys information, but also the way it can be used to add imagery and colour. We were encouraged to read at every opportunity, without prejudice as to subject matter. I have found that use of language, in all its forms benefits from practice, and the reading I did during my schooldays has certainly proved its worth throughout my working life.

History classes were taken by Mr "Tiny" Gatland, a very tall, spare individual, whose lugubrious manner and dry delivery ensured classes seemed to last forever. His lack of any control in class meant that all sessions with him were open season for boys wishing to be disruptive. On occasion though, even Mr Gatland would have had enough, and extra work, or a detention would be awarded to his tormentors. Under his knowledgeable care, we learnt, in great detail, the important aspects of the Bismarck's foreign policy in the closing years of the 19th century, and how this policy, together with the policies and actions of the other European Nations set the scene for the First World War. It is amazing how odd facts still come easily to mind after all this time – the Franco-Prussian War of 1870, the Moroccan Crisis of 1910, "Lebensraum", and the assassination of Austrian Archduke Franz-Ferdinand at Sarajevo. A tie-in with our English studies was the examination of First World War literature from illustrious authors such as Robert Graves and Siegfried Sassoon.

Geography lessons were the province of Mr "Sammy" Severn. A stocky, curly haired individual, Mr Severn had a way of accentuating certain words that ensured we were keen to add our versions of them to the class collection of mimicry. Mr Severn's classes lacked any humour or spontaneity with the consequent result that Geography classes seemed to drag on.

Handicrafts were conducted in an annexe located at the Albany Road/Kingsway junction, a utilitarian building that would not have looked out of place on an Army Camp. This was the lair of Mr "Ronnie" Hanlon. Mr Hanlon was a short individual with a deformity of the spine that made him hunch-backed. A former pupil, he was one of the longest serving members of the teaching staff at Bemrose.

The Societies' Exhibition 1967

He had an uncanny ability to hurl missiles, usually bits of chalk, with deadly accuracy, without appearing to ever take aim. He would take only so much from any boy, then the offender would be grabbed and his tie clamped in a vice! When talking with the younger boys he would impress upon them the need for care when negotiating the roads from main school building to annexe by graphically describing the sounds made if a boy had to be removed from the road after an accident!! Under this crusty exterior however was a man with a genuine interest in teaching.

The sciences were all taught in purpose-built laboratory classrooms. Perhaps the most eccentric of the Science Masters that I associated with was Mr "Baggins" Underwood, a smartly turned out man who had a somewhat "plummy" accent. I assume the nickname "Baggins" was derived originally as a reference from "Lord of the Rings" but I am not sure in which context this was used. Certainly, a surname of "Underhill" would have been an easy association to make. Mr Underwood's chemistry lessons were, to me at least, almost unintelligible. One of my classmates, whose name was Rawlings, was always addressed as "Victor of Hodgkinson!" If this was a clever play on words I never knew; however, it was guaranteed to cause a giggle or two. Theoretical information would be delivered by means of many references to our standard chemistry text book interspersed with jottings on the blackboard. We then had to make sense of this as best we could, often leading to many spectacularly unsuccessful experiments! Out of the Chemistry Lab, Mr Underwood was an enthusiastic musician and often played in the school orchestra.

A single session of Religious Education was held once a week with the Rev Chandler. This gentleman was resplendent in gown and dog collar, his remaining hair providing him with a personal halo that added emphasis to the benevolent looks displayed by so many men of the cloth. His habit of producing whistling sounds when talking provided more raw materials for communal mimicry. He was a devout Christian and whilst he strove mightily to persuade us to see the light, I do not think he was too successful. However, he earned himself a place in Bemrose folklore during a meal one lunchtime when he was overheard to say that the fish dish which he was contemplating eating was "the cod that passeth all understanding"!

Physical Education was pursued at two levels under the watchful eyes of Messrs "Danny" Reece and "Thicky" Goodwin. We had a two periods of PE per week, generally in the Gymnasium, which would usually consist of "Circuit Training", and a double period per week of "Sports". The latter could be any one from Rugby, Football, Cricket, Athletics or Cross Country Running. I remember Cross Country Running with great clarity – getting "stitch" and slowing down to a walk would always be the time when Mr Goodwin would suddenly appear, yelling, "Get moving!" We often used to run a circular course around streets adjacent to the school, whereupon Mr Goodwin would then drive around the course, haranguing the runners from the driving seat of the somewhat elderly Saab car he drove! It was a matter of conjecture as to why he insisted on carrying an old cricket bat in the boot of his car.

Bemrose had a very good and hard earned reputation for sporting excellence. However, those boys that were not particularly adept at any individual sport were rounded up together and whilst they were always given something to do, from the coaching standpoint, they were effectively ignored. Those boys who showed an

aptitude for a sport were coached enthusiastically. I know that there were insufficient resources available for any other system to be used, but I always felt aggrieved – I liked to play cricket, but whatever modest skill I did have was not considered to be good enough to get into the Bemrose coaching system, so my cricket aspirations languished.

Amateur Radio Society at the School Hobbies Exhibition 1967/8
Photo includes Roger Wareham (seated) watched by John Barker, Calvert, Bamford, C P Redfern, Crocker and other visitors. Photo courtesy Derby Evening Telegraph

Dr Chapman and the School Choir 1960

The Librarian was Mr "Bill" Pickering, a gentleman with a noticeable limp, who, according to Bemrose folklore, had gained an injury to the leg during hostilities in World War Two. How accurate this was I don't know, but Mr Pickering certainly had a bad leg, which slowed him down somewhat when in pursuit of boys exhibiting unruly behaviour in the library!!

Mr Goddard was a pale faced man of solemn mien, who rarely hinted that he had any sense of humour. As well as teaching Spanish, he also taught French. I believe the nickname "Pop" was gained one day when he allegedly told the class he was teaching that his 7 year old daughter would be speaking French before them. The nickname was an acknowledgement of fatherhood! During one particular Spanish lesson, we were introduced to the past tense of the verb *ir* – "to go". "Thus," said

Learning Russian with Mr Warwick

Mr Goddard, "'He went' is 'fue', pronounced 'fway'". At this the entire class dissolved into pandemonium. A popular television character of the time was that portrayed by the actor Jack Douglas of a man given to sudden huge twitches, accompanied by the sound "fway!". I distinctly remember seeing Mr Goddard grin although this was quickly masked as he tried to regain order!

There were many characters who did not teach us, but two deserve a passing mention: "Steve" Hindley – was an English Master with a great taste for the theatrical. In the middle of a class he would suddenly jump onto the table, or leap about! As an attention grabber, this succeeded every time! "Siggy" Sowter - a languages master of imposing build - wore suits of impressive weight and thickness as well as big shoes irrespective of season and temperature.

The Later Years

As 1966 slid gently in 1967, our second academic year came around, "3T" became "4T", and school life was now a well practised routine. End of school GCE examinations were an open subject for discussion and debate. Preparatory work was begun in earnest with subject Masters labouring the point that adequate and timely preparation formed the best strategy for examination success. It was too early however to embark upon specific GCE study.

The absence of girls during the normal working day was both a blessing and a curse. It was a blessing because they were not there to distract during the day when we had to work. Conversely, for those boys in a relationship, it was a curse because meetings had to take place away from school. The "disco" culture was in full swing during this time and many happy hours were spent out of school gyrating in dark rooms to the hugely amplified strains of the latest sounds. Trevor East, of "Midlands Today" TV fame was an ex-Bemrosian and he was a DJ at the Friary Hotel in Derby at this time.

This was the time in our lives when the next big adventure started to loom on our horizons – work. I wanted to be a pilot. I knew that learning to fly was going to be an expensive activity so I decided that the best way to pursue this goal was to join the RAF. However, it didn't take me very long into an interview with an RAF Recruitment Officer to realise that my poor grasp of mathematics was not going to be an asset in the pursuit of a flying career in the RAF. I tempered my aspirations to just joining the RAF with transfer to flying later. But as time was to tell, even this lesser aim was doomed to failure.

During 1968, a bicycle ride to Matlock was organised, in which most of the form took part. We all met at the Bus Station in the Morledge, and our route took us through the Market Place, up Irongate and onto the A6, all the way into Matlock. This was before the advent of the infamous Derby Inner Ring Road, and all the one way systems and schemes since. Traffic was much lighter and lorries had not reached the huge size they have today. Consequently, the trip was not as dangerous as it might appear. We straggled along the A6, the strong cyclists at the front occasionally pausing to allow the rest of the red faced, perspiring "snake" to catch up. After an obligatory stop in Matlock Bath, we all came pedalling back, to disperse to our respective parts of Derby. This was good preparation for me because later the same year, Keith Halhead and I cycled to Wrexham, on the Welsh border, to stay with friends. Our enthusiasm departed us for the return trip however; we rode back in the car with my parents, bikes securely tied to the roof!

Our final year in "5T" meant that work for the examinations was now serious. "Mock" GCE examinations were held in November, the results of which dictated which subjects would be taken during the final examinations the following June. Some of us were now old enough to acquire our own transport. The West Gate had a small area set aside for motorbikes and the boys in their fifth year became old enough to invest in such machinery, different models would appear, with great regularity. BSA C15s, Tiger Cubs and early Hondas were parked from time to time alongside the odd moped, Lambretta or Vespa scooter. I knew of no one who had their own car.

By the end of June 1969, the examinations were over and 5T prepared to disband. When the last day of term came around, goodbyes were spoken all round and off we went. When the examination results were published, my results were singularly uninspiring. I was offered the chance to re-take the fifth year and as I had not yet decided what to do as a career, I decided to accept the offer. September 1969 saw me re-installed in 5T, only this time there was a major difference. I was the new boy again, in what had been last years 4T! The Form Master was Mr Hindley, and I thoroughly enjoyed his English lessons and all the capering around! I tried my best that final year, but I fared little better than the first attempt. I left Bemrose School finally in July 1970, to pursue a career in engineering with International Combustion Ltd.

Was it worth it?

I can say most emphatically that it was. Even though the main criterion of academic development for transferring to a Grammar School in the first place was not achieved, I thoroughly enjoyed all my time at Bemrose. I learnt about discipline, both social and personal, and I quickly learned that if something was worth having it was worth waiting for and if necessary, was worth fighting for, but not in the punitive sense. I learned of the traditions within the school and of the anchor they provide. Without traditions to learn from, the wheel is often reinvented a great many times. I felt a sense of pride at being a member of a community of several thousand, from the present day students to those who served in the Second World War.

As I reflect on those far off days in school, I must also compare what has happened since. I have a science degree, I manage my own IT department and I have gained a Private Pilot's licence. The contribution that my time at Bemrose made to these achievements is difficult to quantify. In my experience, it set me on the road to success.

So many of the Masters that laboured so hard and so long trying to impart knowledge to us have now gone to the big school in the sky! I still don't know what has happened to most of my old classmates. But I have to say to Dr Chapman, all the staff and fellows at Bemrose School – thank you.

Under 14 Soccer XI 1967

Tennis Team, May 1966

Basketball Team 1966/67

Rugby XV 1966/7

Athletics Team April 1967

CHAPTER 8

EXTRA CURRICULAR ACTIVITIES

"We Were Bemrose Bucket Bangers"

The School and its Pupils gained a nickname sometime after 1935. Pupils became known as Bemrose Bucket Bangers.

Boys will be boys, and the very act of banning an activity or creating an out-of-bounds area was seen as a challenge to some. This chapter records some of the well remembered events.

Peter Sallis recalls the temptation of visiting the large Fire Service water tank, across Uttoxeter Road. It was decreed that no one should climb up the ladder of the tank, let alone swim in the cool water on a hot summer day! Unfortunately for Peter he was seen by a Prefect and summoned to the Headmaster's study. He suffered six strokes of the cane across the backside and two night's detention.

A summons to the Headmaster's Office was well remembered by Geoffrey Brown, now a doctor in Wales, who fearfully awaited the wrath of Mac, having bought a pair of leather gauntlet gloves from a boy for sixpence (2.5p), not knowing that they were stolen. Another memory was the "Trouser Trick" being played by a lad called Derek Sandford. This would involve a quick flick with the forefinger which opened the fly front of a boy's trousers. They would then have the embarrassment of entering the classroom fumbling to re-button their trousers. Another time Derek stuffed a dead blackbird down the back of Brown's shirt. The teacher could not understand why he was wriggling during the lesson not surprising when there were maggots left behind from the dead bird.

Almost every generation of Bemrose pupils had a few with an ambition to conquer the Green Towers. They were accessed via a spiral staircase, *pictured left* strictly a no-go area. One famous ascent was in 1964 when a bra and panties were flown from the weather vane. The story was featured on the front page of the Derby Evening Telegraph. Another time, the pupils stopped the clock after climbing the ladder to the Clock Tower. All the electrics were exposed, including what looked like a wire with a nail dangling in a bowl of mercury. On another occasion a screwdriver was dropped from the tower, plunging through the ceiling lights and showering a P.E. class below with broken glass. Teacher, Danny Rees, who was almost hit by the screwdriver, looked up and yelled "Boy, you missed, better luck next time!"

Perhaps the most daring Clock Tower incident was in 1969, when a dummy was suspended from the tower. There is a complete photographic record on the school

website which shows exactly how it was done, step by step. It does not, however mention the nightmares suffered by Daisy Fowers, a little girl living opposite the school, who complained that there was a dead schoolboy hanging from the tower.

Today's Student will not even know what inkwells are, but back in "Rubbergob" Trippett's day, the sight in a French class of fifteen inkwells erupting like Vesuvius, after calcium carbide had been added to the ink, left an abiding memory. In 1975, one pupil remembers unscrewing a desk lid and placing a fire extinguisher at the front of the desk. When the unsuspecting victim flung open his desk, the lid fell off and dropped very precisely on to the fire extinguisher, which went off all over the room. Such precision was a source of admiration from the rest of the class, who enjoyed the diversion of clearing up the contents of the extinguisher.

Science lessons were the basis of many pranks and extra mural experimentation. At one time there was a craze to focus the rays of the sun with a magnifying glass on to the desks, in the hope that the desks would catch fire. They never did.

The black pudding trick was rife 1968-70. It consisted of a football sock, filled with left-over rotting food, which was tossed around.

"Poling" sounds an exceptionally cruel tradition, unique to Bemrose School. It involved suspending the victim from a window pole, and leaving them in various locations, sometimes in the long jump pit, another time out of a window, whilst another was suspended across a stairwell. One pupil was "poled" for his birthday being left stranded against the cross bars of the goal post on the football field. It was said that the teachers were only too well aware of this custom, but did nothing to discourage it. It makes birthday bumps sound very tame.

Assemblies were another source of unusual activities. The magnificent grand piano in the Hall was a target, and one prank involved placing drawing pins on the hammers, making it sound like a Honky Tonk. Singing of subtly amended words to hymns or songs has been an activity for many generations. A favourite was "To be a pilchard" as a popular alternative to "To be a pilgrim". Another time, one teacher, nicknamed "Flap", raged at the assembled boys "You in the maroon blazer come to the front" at a time when every boy wore a maroon blazer. "Blob", the Deputy Headmaster Norman Rothwell (who died in 2005), was very strict. He would intone the names of miscreants, followed by the single word "Tower". He then took considerable delight in selecting his tools for corporal punishment.

The long jump pit where victims of "poling" were sometimes left to dangle

Back in the science laboratories *(pictured below)* in 1978 there are memories of strontium 90, a source of radiation, being slipped into the trouser pockets of the lad sitting next to you. Some of Doc Ballard's students ended up in the Derbyshire Royal Infirmary after making sulphur trioxide using hot concentrated sulphuric acid. When the pipe blocked and there was an explosion, the pupils had to be "neutralized" by covering them with bicarbonate. Not surprisingly most of their blazers disintegrated two weeks later. The filling of large polythene bags with gas, before allowing them to float up to the ceiling was another activity. This could be enhanced by flicking them with a lighted match to create an explosion with a quite dramatic effect.

Another unofficial science experiment was to dissolve the inside of blazer pockets using a test tube of iodine crystals. Unplugging the Bunsen burners and then feeding the rubber tubes into another pupils bag, then turning on the gas and lighting with a taper was yet another explosive activity. The explosive properties of sodium would be investigated in class experiments by cutting off tiny slivers and dropping them into a bucket of water. However, one class decided to throw a two inch piece into a tank instead. The resulting explosion smashed the glass tank and covered the laboratory in water. Filling the gas taps with water, smuggling locusts out of the lab and letting them loose in a history lesson are now fond memories.

The Dining Hall continues to give pupils inspiration for mischief. School dinners, with bright red jelly and blancmange with thick synthetic custard would be smuggled out of the refectory. This made a wonderful missile to flick with rulers, the target usually being the ceiling when the plan was to wait until the missiles fell from the ceiling on to the Teacher beneath.

Bonfire nights gave rise to all sorts of mischief, but one pupil was caught in the act by a teacher only seconds after lighting the fuse of a banger. Rather than be caught, he was left with no alternative other than to close his fist over the offending firework - and to save the day, to quickly utter "which b…. threw that?"

Crow scarers were an alternative to fireworks. They could be purchased from a local shop, and had a time delay fuse. The trick was in timing the device to throw the missile into a bin next to the covered playground before escaping to the safety of an adjoining classroom.

Today there is CCTV throughout the school, and so there is virtually no hiding place, and no areas or opportunities to take cover. With electronic registration it is quickly discovered if a pupil is missing from lesson, which means that they are unable to disappear for the afternoon.

Many of the areas favoured by the pranksters are closed to students. The organ loft was a favourite in the 1960's. One prank was to release bean bags or even soapy water from the roof space above the organ loft. Smoking in the organ loft, or even locking other pupils in the loft were regular events. One very sophisticated prank was to hide in the roof space whilst the organ was being played. By lifting the organ pipes and blowing, it would create a dreadful faulty note, which led the player to stop in confusion and then try again, only to experience the same problem. Vibration from the organ could be considerable, and pupils would enter the organ loft to hold the pedal down and make the windows vibrate with the hopes of shattering the glass. It never did.

Bomb scares are not the most original or inventive techniques to gain an afternoon out of the classroom. They are still one of the pranks used today, but it used to be very stupid when pupils used the payphone at the bottom of the school tower to make their calls. It was not very difficult to trace that the call had come from within the school. However, the pupils would be sent off in search of these imaginary bombs, making their search appear more realistic by kicking the satchels lying on the floor and slamming locker doors as loudly as possible.

Static electricity and friction could be used for diversions. The plastic seats in the Language Laboratory would generate static. If you then rubbed your shoes on the carpet and held a compass against the metal headphones, the resultant crackling would spread to every set of headphones.

Highly polished floors could be used to effect too. They could be used to enable desks to slide around in silence, so effecting a place swap without disturbing any work books. When the unsuspecting Teachers turned to write on the board, the desks would glide silently round the room and pupils reappear in different parts of the room.

Woodwork classes were often disrupted when the pupils were subjected to unorthodox punishments. One pupil, who had trouble sawing a joint correctly, spent the whole lesson with the knot of his tie firmly clamped in the vices. The same Teacher had a habit of tying knots in the ties of two miscreants, and when they were only inches apart he would pull them downwards to smack their heads together. The trick of opening woodwork vices to maximum and then placing a boy's hand inside, whilst the person next to him turned the screw one revolution was messy, and would bring down the wrath of "Hunchback" Hanlon.

It was often the Sixth Formers who performed the most sophisticated of pranks. One group would place bets on horses; calling themselves "Fletcher, Walker and Warren Turf Accountants" the maximum bet was 6d (2.5 pence).

Ikey Watts, the Art Teacher was rewarded for his kindness by hiding his teapot, or worse still filling it with all measure of revolting substances.

One pupil remembers being sent out to clear away snow at the front of the school. They decided to try out a little snow sculpture, spelling out the word "umble" - a favourite nickname used by the boys for "Nunky" Norville. In letters three to four feet high, it looked quite startling when viewed from the organ loft.

However, perhaps the cleverest prank was played at the Trans Review. This was always considered the high spot of the term. The Choir were singing in the smarmy style of "Sing Something Simple", but decided to bowdlerise the words with rugby songs. At least half of the audience knew the real words too.

At one Revue, teacher Jim Tate thought to liven up a sketch about the pipe smoking Prime Minister Harold Wilson. It was decided that it might make the pipe smoke seem more realistic if a smoke bomb mixture was used. Unfortunately, he did not expect the pupils to be quite so enthusiastic, and unbeknown to the teacher, the boys spiced up the mixture by 20 times the strength. When Harold lit his pipe, a five foot flame leapt out.

So, to those people who bemoan the youth of today; don't forget that you were all young once.

The Gym

The school labs were scenes of many pranks

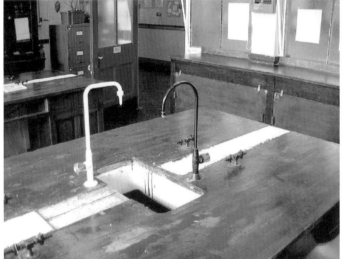

The old toilets served as a 'smoking room'

CHAPTER 9

OLD BEMROSIANS and REUNIONS

There has been an Old Boys' Association since 1913 when it was first formed at the Derby Municipal Secondary School on 1st December. The President in 1924 was Mr L Preston Hewitt. The Old Boys colours were blue and gold until 1930 when the maroon and silver of the new school were adopted and the name was changed to the Old Bemrosian Association. In 1930 there were 60 members paying a subscription of two shillings a year (10p). Pupils were automatically enrolled for a "free" first year following the move to the New Building.

Old Bemrosian ties were available in maroon and silver with a black stripe. The "Buck" from the Park was added later. Cuff links, wraps, sweaters and blazer badges were sold at Townsends, Batties and the Co-op.

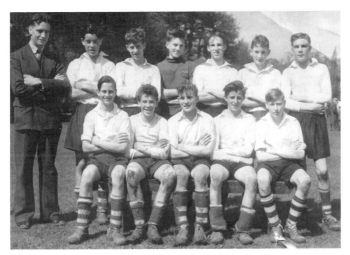

The "Old Bems" held regular meetings, dinners and had their own Dramatic Society. A programme of theatre visits, talks and social evenings culminated in performances of plays at the school. The play performed in 1935 was *She Stoops to Conquer*, when the reunion was

Old Bemrosian Football Club - above 1955, right 1957/8

attended by 200 members. The Old Bemrosian Cricket XI was inaugurated in 1930, with 26 matches arranged. There were also first and second XI Football teams, the first team played in the Midland Amateur Alliance and the second team concentrated on friendly fixtures held at the School. Old Bemrosian rowers entered Derby Regatta.

It became a tradition that the last Saturday of the Christmas term became "Old Boys' Day", held at the school, with a reception, dance and concert.

Major W Smellie, MC, MA, was the inspiration for the Old Bemrosians for 34 years, and his death in 1959 had a significant affect on the Association. By this time annual membership had risen to five shillings (25p), with £2.2s.0d for life membership. It was possible to join the Association for five shillings for a two year subscription when leaving school.

The Association was still very active in 1966 when Mr Harrison took over as Secretary of the Cricket Club and Alan Atkin the Football Club. The team had some success in the M.A.A and the First XI won the M.A.A. Senior cup in 1950, 1952 and 1994; the 2nd XI were undefeated in the league and won the M.A.A. Junior Cup in 1950 and the Division 3 Championship in 1948, 1950 and 1954. In 1970 there were three teams playing in the Midland Amateur Alliance.

OBGA Jubilee Dinner 1980

That same year the Old Bemrosian Golf Society was formed, with the "Bucket Bangers" trophy awarded to the winner of the golf competition. The trophy had been given by Vernon Barnes, who won his own trophy with John Harrington. The Golf Society developed into the Old Bemrose Grammarian Association (OBGA). This has resulted in an annual event in which the golfers meet for the Annual Competition for the Bemrose Bucket Trophy during the day, followed by a dinner for all Members at which the trophy is presented. As many as 100 people have met for the evening event since 1970. With the years passing so the Members pass as well, so that by definition it will come to a "finite" conclusion.

The Old Bemrose Grammarian Association Dinner Menu
May 12, 1981

In November 2002 there was dinner at the Derbyshire County Cricket ground. It had been suggested at the May meeting of the OBGA that another dinner might be held in the winter. The invitation was extended to former pupils of all eras, including the comprehensive and there were hopes of resurrecting the Old Bemrosians Association perhaps in the form of a Bemrose Former Pupils Association (BFPA).

In the event some 35 former pupils attended but none of the post-grammar school era. There was support shown for a BFPA and for the writing of the history. The former is now on the possible list. The latter is a reality. Richard Feist, the Headmaster was to have been the Guest Speaker but had to send his apologies at the last minute. This was a misfortune which deprived those present of hearing his impressive ideas.

As for the OBGA, Geoff Horton, its mainstay for several years, has handed over to Ray Webb. Others are still able to "talk but not do". They rightly feel that it is time for someone younger to take this on. Perhaps this history may be an inspiration.

Old Bemrosian Football Club Dinner 1966

When the change to a Community School came the Head decided that the Old Bemrosians F.C should not continue their long association with the School and so were expected to recruit their players elsewhere. Home matches are still played at

Chester Green, with both 1st and 2nd XI still competing in the Midland Amateur Alliance.

Various reunions take place with mixed results. Alan Robinson had great success in tracing his class of 1942, and a very happy evening was spent at the Gondola Restaurant in Derby. Cliff Billington held a mini reunion at the Rowditch Inn, although only five members of class 5A turned up.

The internet has been used. Peter Farrell, now in Arkansas, set up the very promising site www.bemrose.org. Unfortunately the 9/11 tragedy with the resulting ban on laptops on aircraft has prevented him from maintaining the site as he would have wished. Friends Reunited website also lists Bemrosians trying to locate their old pals.

The school launched www.bemroseschool.org.uk in May 2006.

Bemrose Parent Teacher Association Summer Fair, 7th July 1956
(photo courtesy Derby Telegraph)

Non Fallunt Futura Merentem . Non Nobis Sed Aliis

Pactum Serva . Nil Nisi Bene . Consilio et Animis . Animo et Fide . Semper Audacter

BEMROSE SCHOOL
JUBILEE DINNER
1930 — 1980

7.30 p.m. for 8.00 p.m.
THE PENNINE HOTEL,
DERBY

Saturday 6th September, 1980

*Menu folder for the Parent Teacher Association
Golden Jubilee Dinner 1980*

PART TWO: BEMROSE COMPREHENSIVE AND COMMUNITY SCHOOL (MIXED) 1975-1989

CHAPTER 10

W M WEARNE, 1972 – 83

A Personal View by Tom Kemple

The years in which William Michael Wearne was the Headmaster of Bemrose School would see the biggest change in its history and would affect its future for ever. This awesome change was the introduction of Comprehensive Education. The long established Boys' Grammar School was to be superseded by a mixed sex, mixed ability Comprehensive Secondary School.

Prior to the introduction of the Education Act 1902, all education had to be paid for. This legislation made Primary School Education free but subsequent education had to be paid for. The Education Act 1946 introduced a tripartite education system of Grammar Schools, Secondary Modern Schools and Technical Schools. In reality it was only a two tier system as very few technical schools existed. Entry to Grammar Schools was selective with the 11 plus and 13 plus examinations. Pupils who "failed" went to Secondary Modern Schools. Historically, the Labour Government has always been blamed for the introduction of Comprehensives or more to the point abolishing Grammar Schools. However, this policy of mixed ability was also supported by Conservative Governments. The policy of the 1960s gradually became fact in the 70s.

Michael Wearne was born and bred in Camborne, Cornwall. I do not know what year and have not the courage to write back and ask him. I may have got away in the past calling Martin Bull and John by their Christian names but no way will I ask Mr Wearne his age! After leaving Launceston College in 1945 he joined the army, "a quaint custom of the time" as he said in a recent letter (27.1.05) to me. He took his PGCE at Kings College, Newcastle an outstation of Durham University. His first teaching post was at Botelar Grammar School, Warrington, followed by the public school Rossall near Fleetwood. After seven years and having been turned down for various Headships he looked abroad and was soon appointed Head of the Anglo-Colombian School in Bogota, Colombia. It was a co-educational school of

700 pupils between seven and eighteen. With nearly all Colombians but with some ex-pats as well it had the backing of the British Council which recruited the 12 British teachers from the United Kingdom. After seven years he felt that although fluent in Spanish and immersed in the culture, he was a foreigner and recognised that this would always be the case and returned to Britain. Here he felt a stranger again as the country had changed so much since he left. He had by then acquired a son, wife and daughter. Jobless, he applied for several positions including Queen Elizabeth's, Ashbourne. He was successful at the next, Bemrose. He recalls walking up the drive noting the driveway and architecture and felt he should apply for the Caretaker's job instead. This then was the start. The end was his retirement in 1983.

On his appointment he had possibly the hardest act to follow in succeeding Dr Chapman. I feel that it is fair to say that Mr Wearne did not inspire the same respect as Head that 'The Cheese' had. This was because he was the first of the generation of Heads who were more administrators than teachers. Reading through 11 years of reports that he presented to the Governors, administration must have taken up most of his time. I can recall only very rare occasions such as when there was a Teachers' strike that he was in the classroom. In his defence he had on-going battles with the Education Authority both Local and County, on such basics as heating the school to an acceptable temperature.

As in any good pantomime, there has to be a villain who you can hiss at. Michael Wearne was perfect for the part. He followed Dr Chapman, a long serving much respected Head. He was to be the architect of the demise of Bemrose as a Grammar School. A great challenge was undoubtedly having to combine two widely different schools - Bemrose and Rykneld - into one "Comprehensive" unit. The decision to make Bemrose a Comprehensive was out of his hands. More than a few teachers were against the idea. The pupils at Bemrose did not want to be a Comprehensive and I am sure that our contemporaries at Rykneld did not wish to join with us. Geographically it made sense although since time immemorial, there had been at least one pitched battle per year between the two schools.

Later in correspondence with me and others, Michael Wearne revealed he was a whole hearted advocate of Comprehensive Education and brooked no criticism of the system or his implementation of it. He admitted in a report to the Governors at the time "that reduced intellectual content in courses will lead to frustration on the part of staff whose proportion of graduates is well above the national average". In the same report he states that they have had to tread delicately in an attempt to achieve some improvement in the conduct of older Rykneld pupils without causing resentment which would be counterproductive. He did not forsee that the frustrations that he mentioned would lead to at least three physically strong Masters suffering nervous breakdowns.

The Authority only provided two days training for the Rykneld staff while for his own even less. There was virtually no attempt by the Authority to find out what it all entailed. It was mainly down to the staff to find out for themselves. The Local Education Authority and County Council enforcing this system seemed to rely on the ideology of the time rather than logistics.

Rykneld School Staff – many joined Bemrose when the schools combined

The initial plan was to leave the two schools as they were with Bemrose being the Upper School and Rykneld the Lower School. This entailed some Masters having to perform the Bemrose dash from Upper to Lower or vice versa. Fine at lunch time, but really only suitable for the younger fitter Masters in breaks between classes. When the National Union of Teachers held a 'work to rule' a Staff Union member would arrange for taxis whilst their non-union colleagues still had to walk.

Along with the mixed ability came pupils from totally different catchments areas and backgrounds. Previously the intake was mainly from Allestree, Mackworth and parts of Littleover. Whole generations of families went to the same school, often many siblings following their father. The intake now was from the less well off areas of Normanton with no tradition of going to a school such as Bemrose. From these areas with varying degrees of social problems, the pupils brought problems which the Staff had never had to deal with before. Discipline, always strict, began to erode. The number of expulsions and suspensions began to rise steadily, culminating in an incident in 1978 when a parent of an expelled pupil came to school and physically attacked the Head.

These comments are not idle speculation but can be seen in the Governors' Reports held in the Records Office at Matlock. Was this the fault of Comprehensive Education or the decline of society which seems to have continued unabated since?

The House system in the school was retained. This was at the insistence of staff, who believed that the House structure encouraged older boys to accept responsibility. That the House system was a throw back to the Public School way of life raises the question whether Comprehensive Education cherry-picked the best bits of the Grammar School Education but without the Grammar.

Returning to the point about "reduced intellectual capacity", certainly at Speech Day we were surrounded by Masters in gowns and hoods. We had two Doctors teaching Chemistry, David Ballard and Bernard Hawley. Another Doctor was David Johnson the Music Teacher. Occupying a prefab next to the Refectory he managed with the minimum of resources to instil a love of classical music. He is still assistant organist at Derby Cathedral. With Peter Bateman and Bernard Hawley they were the backbone of the School Orchestra.

From an all male perspective, the most obvious change was that the school now had girls. Sadly from my point of view this came in my last two years – too late to have any bearing on my academic or social life at the school. The girls were taken into the lower school and the first intake did not move to the upper school until the fourth year by which time I was long gone.

Of course having girls presented its own logistical problems. Women teachers for subjects such as PE had to be specially recruited. Mrs Dawn Johnson was one of the first and was married to the teacher who coached the Derby Borough Schools side. Amenities in two 'all boys' schools had to be adapted for use by girls. In defence of Mr Wearne, it seemed to be a running battle with the Education Authorities in order to provide these basic facilities. Again this is not idle speculation but is documented in Governors' meeting. Another problem was that while some teachers' ideas of discipline were considered the norm for a boys' school, attitudes had to change when dealing with the fairer sex.

Bemrose School as it had been known actually ceased to be a "Comprehensive" in 1988. All Masters were required to tender for their own jobs and a new school called 'Bemrose Community School' was born. The old School as such ceased to be in all but the building and memory. Bemrose has been described as giving "the privilege of a Public School Education for free". So when looking back at what Bemrose is and what it is now with Special Measures in the recent past and reduced intellectual results it is not the school that was the Grammar School, it is a totally different entity and as such should not be mourned for today. Michael Wearne has since described the rumblings of old pupils as "useless repining". This to an extent is true, it is gone, but such an off-hand comment does away with the feeling of tradition and belonging that many pupils had and have watched the demise of a one time great School.

One ex-master was tackled about the lack of success in league tables which showed Bemrose to be at the bottom. Whilst not defending it he said that it was relative how you judged success. If the number of Oxford and Cambridge entrants was down then that is one way but a lot of pupils now joined the school who could neither read nor write. If at the end of their time they had a basic education and could read and write was that not also success? In the first year of the Comprehensive intake to the Lower School, there was a remedial class where sixth formers from the upper school would donate one of their free periods a week to helping with the class.

My memories of the School are legion, mostly good but with the odd bad one. Thirty five years' hindsight lends a rosy tint to even the strongest bifocals.

At one stage I and other colleagues had by ways nefarious made copies of the master keys to the school - an untold treasure indeed. We thought we were being highly original having coffee from a primus stove in the roof over the physics lab dark room. Only to find when the Bemrose website (bemrose.org) appeared that we were by no means the first to do this – every generation seemed to have a set of keys. Climbing into the Clock Tower via the roof over the glass ceiling of the hall took some nerve but not as much as climbing the outside and erecting a dummy from the weathervane. On one of the rafters above the Hall is written in chalk "Speech Day - the last anachronism" by some latter day anarchist.

The one thing that stands out more than any thing else in my time is the teachers. Some terrified us. One Danny Rees was outstanding; he terrified everybody. However, his love and enthusiasm for sport and especially rugby was legendary. Like all Welshmen of that era he was said to have had a trial for Wales. But only a few knew was that before playing for Derby Rugby Club, he was a regular first team scrum half for Leicester Tigers. This came to light when the man who poached him from Leicester told me when looking at a team photograph at Derby RFC. Another little known fact was that he was fluent in German, a skill he obtained whilst in the armed services.

He flew relief supplies in to Berlin on the Airlift, the biggest humanitarian exercise ever held at the time where the British and Americans flew supplies into Berlin for 11 months in 1948 to overcome the Soviet blockade. The initial reaction by me and others to whom I have mentioned it was, "Bloody hell, he _could_ play a bit then". It was a brave boy who sniggered when he demonstrated vaulting over a horse in the gym and his pens, keys, and loose change flew all over the place. Danny was mainly rugby, cricket and the gym whilst John 'Thicky' Goodwin was football and athletics. The fact that they both taught Geography gave the subject a certain amount of respect but we inferred that it must have been an easy degree to get.

Peter 'Flapp' Bateman helped with rugby. He was a Classics Master in the Macfarlane model. Ancient History, Ancient Greek and Latin were his main subjects. He had more than a passing interest in the French Horn which could be heard regularly reverberating around the top corridor. He deliberately came to school early to practise so that he would not disturb his neighbours in his cottage at Winster. He organised sponsored walks by Bemrose Rugby Club from Duffield or wherever to his cottage in Winster. There at the end of 20 or so miles he would put on supper before transporting us in shifts to Matlock railway station and home. We

Under 14 Athletics Team – City Champions 1980
with teacher Fran Harlow

City Champions 1980 Under 13 Athletics Team with teacher Fran Harlow

would be allowed into the basement of the cottage to play with his collection of Victorian arcade machines. With the introduction of Comprehensive Education, the writing was on the wall for his subjects and he was to teach Religious Education as the Classics were phased out. Ultimately he left to be a peripatetic teacher of the French Horn.

Back to sport, in later years John Davis (Leeds United supporter who preferred rugby league), Brian Walker (played in the same teams as several of the protégés later at Derby RFC) and 'Frankie' Vaughan all contributed to inter-house and school rugby. Craig Cunliffe, all five foot something (but not a lot) was into football and cricket. Martin Bull did football, cricket and basketball. Sadly he died very young being struck on the chest playing cricket in a local league. David 'Pedro' Amedro was a good cricketer and was always the starter at Sports Day. After his premature death his obituary in the Derby Evening Telegraph revealed that after leaving University he was head-hunted by one of the secret services. Perhaps he was the starter as he was the only one they could trust with a gun? Certainly if his aim with a gun was as true as with a piece of chalk or a board rubber, the defence of the realm was in safe hands.

Bemrose first year rugby team 1972-73.
(Left to right) Back row Mr. Bateman (Flap), Neil Barker, Charlie Cotterill, Andy Pyle, Philip Rubini, Gerald Heelan. *Middle Row* Sean Hardingham, Paul Sweeting, Phillip Savage, Jonathon Wilkinson, John Kenyon. *Front Row* Darren Parker, Alan Jones, Dean Masters, Chris Ellison, Steve Clark, John Sadler, John Harm

Having only ever participated in rugby and athletics - i.e. throwing things - I may be doing teachers who willingly helped out at cricket, tennis, cross country or basket ball a disservice. There were other clubs and organisations that teachers were involved in. Mr Marshal ran the Christian Fellowship before leaving for the

Bemrose 2nd year cricket team c1971-72?

(Left to right) **Back row:** *Mick Perkins, Yan Ziborski, Kevin Dutton, Phillip Reilly, Bob Dixon, Craig Richardson, Nick Reynolds.* **Front Row:** *Graham Reiter, Nick Hindley, Mr Calvert (Pobble), Dave Chambers, Gary Hammond.*

Photograph and names kindly provided by Gary Hammond - Thanks Gary. Thanks to Tom Kemple for the missing names.

Bemrose 4th year rugby team 1974-75

(Left to right) **Back row** *Dave Fowers, Tank ?, Mick Perkins, Sean Coyle, Richard Pye, Andrew Hill, ? Clarke, 'Frankie' Vaughn.* **Front Row** *Gary Southall, Steve Whitbread, Graham Wright, Graham Adkin, Andy Franick, Nick Denton, ? Clarke*

Photograph and names kindly provided by Dave Fowers - Dave Wildgoose has provided additional help with the names.

church. Religious Education was taught variously over my years by two ordained ministers Mr Thistlewood – "Pinhead" due to his extraordinary thinness - and Mr Chalmers, known as 'Whistler'. Dr Chapman who was a Sidesman and Lay Reader at Derby Cathedral used to step into the breech when necessary. The Archaeological Society was run by Mr Willets. No-one can forget the philatelic club and the wild frenzy each year of the stamp auction all organised by 'Pobble' Calvert. French exchanges by 'Ossie' Osbourne, long before the other pretender who nicked his surname and sang in Black Sabbath. German exchanges were arranged by Mr Dorrell, Youth Hostelling and American exchanges by "Noddy" Nadin.

"Noddy" is still going strong with an almost photographic memory backed up by legions of records of every form he taught. He also taught in America on a sabbatical from Bemrose. His records of Youth Hostelling trips reveal as many as 68 pupils on some trips. He was ably abetted by Masters such as Blake, Bull and Davies. Of course, with the latter two I would wager that there was no distance to speak of between any given hostel and the local hostelry. I should imagine "Noddy" probably has the biggest collection of Noddy memorabilia outside the Enid Blyton Trust all donated by grateful pupils over the years.

These activities were of course in our own time or in school holidays. Somehow I cannot see it happening today. Certainly not without a plethora of forms by the Local Authority, risk assessments, and child protection issues backed up by the compensation culture if anything went wrong. Of course many of these activities were features both before and after my time. Some of the personnel may have changed between Headships but I cannot recall ever playing on a Saturday morning or training after school where teachers were not present. They were always there. I found out later from "Noddy" Nadin that Danny Rees drew up rotas and every master took his turn. Many turned up anyway. That is not to decry their successors but just to emphasise how fortunate in hindsight we were at that time.

What struck you about the teachers was that some of them seemed to have been there forever. In 'Jake' Harbach's case it was nearly true as having joined Bemrose at its inception he stayed until his retirement. Martin Bull, Ian Blake, John Nadin and Bernard Hawley were all Old Bemrosians who returned to teach. The teachers never seemed to leave; if one did it was a shock. Contrast this with

Philip Thomas, Bernard Hawley and John Nadin. Bernard and John returned to teach at Bemrose.

121

Michael Wearne's reports to the Governors in later years when there appeared to be staff leaving on a regular basis.

Sadly, Danny, Thicky, Flap and Pedro and others are no longer with us. The passage of time is cruel in that you think you will always see them one more time just to say thanks. In the last year (2005), Mr Shaw and Mr Rothwell have passed away along with Miss Blaine, all well into their eighties.

My memories of Bemrose more or less finish when I left in 1977 after a monumentally undistinguished time academically but with representative honours for both rugby and athletics. I enjoyed myself. Three visits were paid to the school in the successive years for the Old Boys against the School 1st XV match. These were usually one sided affairs as I realised having played for the school side in the two years previous to leaving school. It was really a case of men against boys but a certain amount of champagne rugby was played or to be more accurate, 'Bass' rugby as the team meeting was held in the Junction Tavern beforehand to discuss tactics and see where five props could fit into the team. The Old Boys were made up of a few years cobbled together and most played for either University or Club sides so the result was always inevitable. The debrief took place back at the Junction always joined by a few of the masters willing to renew acquaintances or just to get a drink at 4.30pm. This was in the days before all day opening and delicate negotiations had to be opened some weeks before to find suitable premises. There was for a brief time a Staff against the 1st XV match but this was abandoned by edict from the Local Education authority as they sometimes turned into wars of attrition.

To use another Rugby metaphor for the last time, Jim Telfer on the eve of a Lions International said to the team that if they won they would form an unbreakable bond which if they met in the street 20 years later would still be as strong.

Evidence of this was seen a few weeks past when two members of my form, one who I see regularly and the other infrequently, met for the first time in at least 30 years. Conversation flowed; histories were caught up with, people asked about, and families compared. There was the common bond of Bemrose pupils.

One of the First Girls by Leanne Bell

I was 11 when I started in what was then called the Lower School.

I am one of those whose memory fades over details some 20 years ago! But I do remember my friends and I feeling very "lost". We were the first girls to attend the school and being surrounded by boys we just had to set an example. We were very well looked after and somewhat "respected" for being in a unique position.

My lasting impression of those first days was the "yucky" burgundy coloured pinafore dresses we were expected to wear. As the first females in the school we would have appreciated a more "fetching" design and colour for us to parade in. As I got older, I and many others decided that we would prefer to wear traditional black, grey and white – skirts, blouse, t-shirt, sweatshirt, woolly socks etc., and not the School burgundy. In any case it clashed with my auburn hair!

Girls at Bemrose School 1978

I was a keen cross-country runner and as a result achieved some early notoriety. Races started from the School Grounds and went into the very hilly local recreation ground at the bottom of the St. Albans Road - I recall three races in which I came 5th, 8th & 11th. In one of these I became so hot that I ripped off my wrap-around skirt and continued the race in my lovely big grey school PE knickers. My picture appeared in the School Magazine and it took sometime to live the incident down!

Fourth year Cross Country Runners 1971

In 1977 when I was 13 we moved up to the Upper School on Uttoxeter Road. Our form room was a "terrapin" outside at the back of the school.

Upper School seemed so much larger than the Lower School and seemed full of male pupils in all years and particularly in the Sixth Form. Along with the other girls this was probably the first time we had really noticed the other sex. Although some of us were "villains", like many teenagers of the time, we were "angels" compared to others.

Lessons were in classrooms along the main corridor fronting the huge playing fields. The outside wall was completely glazed and the room became very hot in the summer months. Later we had cookery and needlework lessons in the newly built extensions to the school in the form of square brick buildings just down the slope at the back right of the school. The rooms were very modern and we enjoyed using all the new equipment.

I recall 2 members of staff. Mr Dingley was a kindly man, much respected by the pupils; as I am only about 5'4" his very broad and tall build made a lasting impression on me, even now when I see him occasionally in town. He was very good to us. Mr Allison was a young, trendy English teacher with whom we had lots of fun; he was drooled over by many of us teenage girls.

Two memories of school were the queues waiting to see the "nit nurse" – hoping not to get shown up by having her put us to one side for a further look – as we may have the insects roaming around in our heads, and visits to the toilets where it was normal to be asked if we had any "fags".

I recall incidents with friends near the end of my school time. Once we were bored and decided to take a walk into the Town Centre along the main Uttoxeter Road. Unfortunately we happened to bump into a Teacher so our little trip was cut short! Another time we took a short cut to St Albans Road and down to the park to have a crafty menthol fag with a few friends. An unlikely scenario was skipping a maths lesson and creeping into my friends' lesson where I wouldn't be recognised by the temporary teacher who was covering.

Over my time at school my interest in sport and PE took precedence over academic subjects. It was my good fortune to attend a school where we were able to use the extensive playing fields and tennis courts. Nevertheless I have been reasonably successful since leaving school which must reflect the excellence of the teaching we received even if we did not appreciate it at the time!

The Famous 1975 School Photograph
in its entirety and then in sections at a larger size

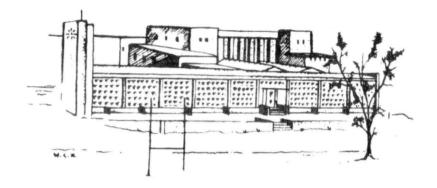

Line drawings of upper and lower schools

Bemrose 1st XI Soccer Team
winners of Shentall Cup 1980/81

The front path up to the School door
Photo courtesy Andy Savage www.derbyphotos.co.uk

CHAPTER 11

R L HOBSON, 1983-93

Robert Hobson MA (Cantab.) was appointed head of a thriving and over subscribed Comprehensive School in 1983.

In September 1984 there were more than 1,150 pupils and 69 teaching staff. 75 Pupils were in the 6th form, and the Lower School was at Bedford Street on the site now used by the Bishop Lonsdale Primary School. It was home to Years 1 and 2, which would now be known as Years 7 and 8. Upper School was the main building on Uttoxeter New Road, and housed Years 3 to 6. The planned admission in 1985 was to be limited to 220.

During his ten years as Head Teacher the school was re-organised and the 6th form disbanded. However, the school remained popular with 800 pupils and 50 staff.

The aims of the School, as stated by Robert Hobson, were to make it possible for children to become happy and successful individuals who accept responsibility for their community, for society and for all its members. "We aim to help them understand themselves and their fellows from differing backgrounds. We aim for excellence in every field of human endeavour: and we work closely with parents to create acceptable codes of conduct and behaviour. We stress the need for hard work and self discipline. We try to discover and develop talent, and to remedy weaknesses".

The school was organised in a Year system, with each Year having a Year Head supported by a Deputy. These members of staff were primarily responsible for the welfare and progress of the pupils from the start of their school career at Bemrose. The Year Head would move through the School with the pupils and so was the first point of contact should there be any problems.

The School continued to be divided into four Houses: Burke, Newton, Sidney and Wellington. Members of a family would always be placed in the same House. Under the leadership of House Heads, many social, sporting, musical and dramatic events were held.

The School Uniform was maroon and white, but members of the 6th form were allowed to wear grey suits.

With such a large number of students on three sites (the Albany Road annexe was used for practical subjects) it was possible to offer a choice of 14 A level subjects to the 40 pupils in the upper Sixth. 238 pupils in the Fifth Year chose from a range of 21 different O level subjects, as diverse as Polish and Woodwork, or opt for C.S.E. from a list of 24 subjects including such things as Automobile Engineering Science, Typewriting or Food and Nutrition. The range of the curriculum was undreamt of before reorganisation. The Pastoral Care System developed out of all recognition. Exam results improved, year on year, from 1985.

Bemrose becomes a Community School

In the late 1980's all the schools in Derby were re-organised again when the Government decided that schools should manage their own budgets under a system known as Local Management of Schools. All Secondary School Heads underwent a period of preparation for their new Community School status, leaving the every day running in the hands of an acting Head Teacher. Vincent Henderson, who first joined Bemrose in 1975, just as the school was about to be merged with Rykneld Secondary school to become a Comprehensive School, stepped into this role.

The reorganisation of Derby Secondary Schools caused much local comment, in the press and elsewhere. One constant refrain was the objection to change itself. Robert Hobson commented that people still say "I remember Bemrose when it was a proper school".

However, many secondary age children passed through the school after his appointment in 1983. Few of those children knew that Bemrose had been a Boys' Grammar School before 1975. Local folklore has it that Bemrose stopped being a good school when it became a Comprehensive. However, the facts show that exam results were improved. The accommodation, equipment and resources are still as good as anywhere in the County.

Change may be threatening to some people, but Robert Hobson reminded us that the fundamental philosophy that all pupils are of equal value, and the belief in firm discipline, hard work and above all the importance of good relationships between the Staff and Pupils made a School the City of Derby could be proud of. "It is a Community Comprehensive which believes in achieving excellence, just as much as the Grammar School did. The difference is that we believe everyone can achieve, whatever their age or background."

1987 Staff signatures

Robert Hobson and Bemrose School were ready for the 1990's. The "new" Bemrose Community School (BSC) opened on 6th September, 1989, as a <u>Co-educational</u> Comprehensive maintained by Derbyshire County Council. There were 685 pupils, with 140 new First Years from 15 Junior Schools.

Expectations were high, with an understanding of the value that a good education may bring: stretching the mind, enriching the spirit and exercising the body. The pupils were expected to learn hobbies, interests and activities from good teachers. "Students need the right qualifications and experiences to enjoy fulfilling and well paid careers in later life."

Robert Hobson said at the time:
"BCS is the centre of its community: we have much to offer to everyone in our area, and we have much to learn from those who live and work near us. The School itself is a community too. Our students will learn to live together in harmony with others. They will discover the need for hard work. They will learn the importance of discipline and self discipline. We shall work hard together for a common goal; the education of young people and the whole community. All of us at BCS will work to help our pupils achieve excellence - we shall expect from them a determination to succeed by their own efforts, by good attendance, by punctuality, by sensible behaviour. Parents have the right to expect much of the teachers. What do teachers have the right to expect of parents? Simply this - send your children to school well dressed, properly equipped, with clear instructions to work hard and

behave properly. If we work together for the good of the children, then they will succeed at school."

Official Opening of new Art, Design and Technology Block
on September 28th by Margaret Beckett MP

In the Summer of 1990, a major building programme was finished, providing new kitchen and dining facilities, enlarged design and technology accommodation and specialist provision for drama, dance and music. The building project cost £1.3 million, and enabled the three sites which had been used since 1975 to be combined on one site. The library was refurbished and the school driveway extended. The new facilities were opened by Margaret Beckett M.P. on 27th September 1990.

Robert Hobson was proud of the school's rich and balanced curriculum. It offered both arts and technology and enabled young people to develop a range of skills needed in today's complex world. The future for all was excellent. The School was particularly well resourced for students with language or learning difficulties. All students took part in a work experience programme. The well qualified and creative staff were determined to maintain a firm but welcoming atmosphere. A talented teaching force offered pupils and their parents the opportunity to achieve the highest educational standards within a disciplined framework.

Governors controlled their own £1m budget, deciding their own financial priorities. With continued Local Authority support, the links with local employers would be further developed, ensuring that school leavers were equipped for success in the job market.

1990's Staff. Back row: –, Val Watson, –, Rob Lewis, Bob Le Brocq, –, John Davies
Front row: Eunice McCutcheon, Chris Collier, Pat Savage, Joan Hewitt, Vic Green,
Malcolm Morgan, Fran Harlow, Bran Hicks

1990's Staff
Val Watson, John
Davies, Joan Hewitt,
Fran Harlow
Rob Lewis,
Steve Shackleton,
Vic Green,
Malcolm Morgan.

There was an upsurge of schools opting for Grant Maintained status. Many felt that this would create extra money, which the schools would administer directly without Local Education Authority intervention. However, the general feeling of the Governing Body was that Bemrose had fared well through Council control, and there was no wish to jump on the bandwagon of Grant Maintained status.

The School continued to work well through 1992. Much effort went into collecting books to send to schools in Bosnia, after one of the staff had observed the chronic lack of resources there. A massive container was despatched, containing many books which had been collected by the School after an appeal in the local newspaper.

Other events included a school trip to Osnabruck and a mock General Election. The school play was Harold Pinter's "The Birthday Party" and there was a "Summer Serenade" Concert. Spring Term brought an excellent production of "Oliver". Val Watson, as Director, involved staff as well as students. Her casting caused amusement when teachers took such parts as Mr Bumble and Fagin.

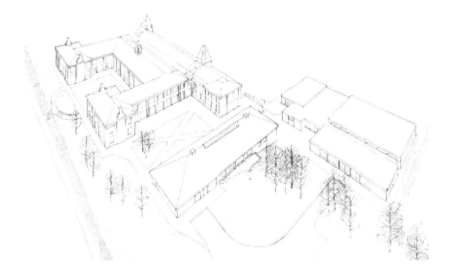

Line drawing of School and 1990 extension

Staff of Lower School prior to re-organisation

Records of Achievement were introduced, which would monitor a pupil's progress throughout their school career. These were likely to be used when applying for college or employment, as proof of what had been achieved during five years at Bemrose School.

In March 1993 there were sensational headlines in the local newspaper when two students were expelled. It would now be called permanent exclusion. There had been a fight outside school, and claims that "worried parents at a trouble torn Derby School are too frightened to send their children to school because of race violence, and the pupils claiming that they live in fear of thugs at the school".

Staff in July 1993

A spokesman for the County Council defended Mr Hobson as very experienced and able to deal with the situation.

However by the end of May, Mr Hobson had decided to resign at the end of the Summer Term, and return to the classroom as an English teacher at St. Benedict's School, Darley Abbey. Again the Derby Telegraph ran banner headlines, attributing his resignation to the criticism from parents for losing control during the race hate attacks at the school. Mr Hobson refused to discuss his reasons for resigning – four candidates were interviewed for the Headship.

Ironically next month the same newspaper was heralding the School for its inclusion among 320 listed in the "Parents Choice" supplement of the *Independent on Sunday* newspaper, after being nominated by parents and checked by education specialists.

By then it was too late.

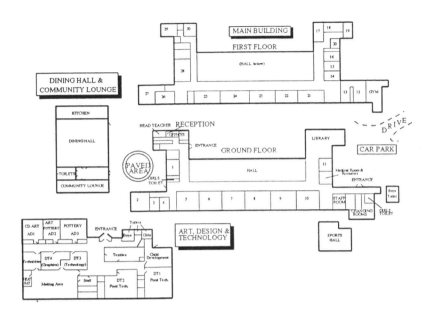

A £1.3 million major building programme replaces all three sites

New Dining Hall and Community Lounge
© *Picturethepast and used by permission*

Late Autumn morning on the playing fields
Photo courtesy Andy Savage www.derbyphotos.co.uk

CHAPTER 12

ROBERT KENNEY, 1993 – 97

The Governing Body was inundated with applications for the Headship of the Community School to replace Robert Hobson in 1993. Interviews for the Headship lasted for three days, with the final session becoming quite a marathon when the panel could not agree their choice from the four candidates shortlisted. Eventually Kevin Hepworth, Chair of Governors, offered the post to Robert Kenney.

Robert Kenney was aged 39 when he joined the School and the youngest Head Teacher ever to be appointed at Bemrose School. He was married, with a young family, including twin daughters Isobel and Alison, then aged six and a son Joe (five). He lived in Castle Donington.

With a Masters Degree in Education, he left his post as Deputy Head of Haywood Comprehensive School, Nottingham to take on the headship of Bemrose School. A young man obviously full of ideas from his time at Haywood, he irritated some staff and enthused others by frequent reference to his previous experience.

Within a relatively short time he introduced an Equal Opportunities policy to counteract the perceived problem of racism, a successful anti-bullying strategy, a "Special Educational Needs" policy affecting many pupils and a Sex Education Policy.

In 1994 the school hit rock bottom, when its examination results were the second lowest in the county. This was no surprise to Mr Kenney who had already taken remedial action to deal with the problem.

His next action was to improve the school environment with a programme of redecoration and structural alterations. The reception area was moved from the administration area to near door 5 into what was originally the prep room 8. Not surprisingly this action was openly criticized by many staff and parents, who considered that the money would be far better spent on employing additional staff.

Ignoring this typical public reaction, he now brought in his financial expertise. The school accounts showed a deficit, and for the first time in the history of the School, the prospect of making teachers redundant was mooted. The Teaching Unions were advised, and voluntary redundancy offered to several Teachers after the relevant notification had been issued.

Kenney was very successful in gaining funding from outside agencies. The Princes Trust, Derby Pride, Theatre in Education and Local Industry all contributed, especially in Careers Guidance, Work Experience Opportunities, and the supply of computers. A Home Office Section 11 grant was secured to support students with learning problems, the money being used to convert the original Woodwork Room into a Computer Suite. The improvement in IT facilities was much appreciated. A Task Force grant in excess of £35,000 was obtained, together with TVEI and ROSPA grants. "Education for All" supplied Specialist Teachers and resources to the school. A marketing working group was started with the idea of promoting the school.

Head teacher Robert Kenney (seated) with Deputy Heads Sandra Fletcher and Vic Green. December 1997

The face-lift went ahead, but had an unexpected outcome. When Fire Officers visited the site to sanction the provision of lockers for the pupils' personal belongings they discovered that the upstairs corridor had no fire escape from the first floor West Wing. This led to it being closed off instantly. Only a hasty re-rooming prevented the whole school being shut down. Subsequently, Derbyshire County Council authorised a £30,850 brick built fire escape which gave access to the Car Park.

An After School Study Club, with staff and transport provided for students wishing to stay after school, was especially popular. Some students stayed in the Library to finish their homework.

Arts, Music and Drama were developed, with the pupils presenting a Music Festival, and some excellent musical and drama productions including "Bugsy Malone" and "Joseph". "Sport for All" created exceptional team and sporting endeavour. There was a trip to Paris.

It was not surprising that the pupils did not see the Head Teacher except at Assembly time. It was clear that he knew what he was doing and worked exceptionally hard to rectify problems, particularly those which prevented the pupils from making good progress. His experience at Haywood as Deputy was paying off now that he was in charge.

He had a friendly and sociable nature which was appreciated by both teaching and office staff. The office staff, on whose hard work his efforts depended, have especially fond memories of his warmth and humour. It was not unusual for him to make the afternoon tea. He joined in several staff functions. An evening at the Greek Taverna in Derby, graced by a belly dancer and concluding with the traditional pot smashing will be long remembered.

In 1996, the School was notified that there was to be a full Ofsted Inspection. Staff attended various inset meetings in preparation. Parents were invited to complete a questionnaire expressing their opinions of the school. A Public Meeting was well publicised, but the inspection team had not anticipated the level of parental apathy when only two attended the open meeting. A record low for anywhere in the country!

The Inspection took place from September 23rd - 27th, 1996. A team of 12 Inspectors sat in on over 180 lessons. The report was anxiously awaited.

The Inspector Mrs Sylvia Richardson concluded overall that the school was giving less than satisfactory value for money, with a higher than average unit cost. This was despite there being 45 teaching staff for the 683 pupils, a ratio which would be envied by many more privileged private schools.

The lack of vocationally orientated courses, high number of exclusions and poor attendance figures revealed a school with serious weaknesses. The Management Team Structure was considered top heavy and a review was initiated. Other adverse comments included 25% of the teaching observed was judged less than satisfactory, and the lack of support from the parents particularly the low turn out at Parents' Evenings was noted. The PFTA (Parents, Friends and Teachers Association) had earlier been abandoned due to lack of interest.

More serious was the shortfall in time being spent actually learning and teaching. Every week there was 1 hour 40 minutes less than the recommended time being spent in the classroom. Over a full school year this was considerable. The timetable was hastily extended.

There were however complimentary points too.

Robert Kenney was praised for his leadership, despite the comment that this had not yet had much impact on the central issue of achievement. The Curriculum was examined in detail, and the Personal and Active Learning (PAL) Department highly praised for its relevant and well planned course. This has since been replaced with a PSE (Personal and Social Education) course. One remark about there being "virtually no litter" was met with amusement by those who had witnessed a very Senior Member of Staff, scouring the school and grounds with a black bin liner to hand. His dedication as Senior Litter Picker, the like of which had never been witnessed before amazed his colleagues. Unfortunately, the students did not get the message and the litter soon returned after the inspection.

In November 1996, the local newspaper reported "a school with one of the worst track records in Derby has been given a glowing report from the independent watchdogs" and stated that "Robert Kenney is delighted".

Robert Kenney moved to Holgate Comprehensive School, Hucknall, Nottingham in 1997 after only three and a half years at Bemrose Community School. His time was then the shortest of any Head Teacher at Bemrose School.

New computer suite, financed by the Home Office

● Winning team ... competition winners Shamila Rashid (11) and Mumtaz Begum (14) with the Mayor of Derby Robin Wood, new head Robert Kenney and bookweek organiser Ros Litting.

School gets a taste of Japan

PUPILS at a Derby secondary school turned Japanese for a week to mark a book-reading festival.

Bemrose Community School, in Uttoxeter New Road, got a taste of the Orient during National Children's Bookweek.

Events included learning about Oriental art such as origami, karate, Japanese calligraphy, cooking and music.

"It was absolutely wonderful. It's been standing room only for all the events," said librarian Marilyn Thompson.

More than 200 children also took part in a Japanese general knowledge quiz. But the main aim of the week was to encourage children at the school to read more.

● Bookworms ... Emma Sloman holds the certificate with Tony Hurd and other pupils.

National Children's Book Week 1993
(Photos courtesy Derby Evening Telegraph)

John Davies presents a cheque in memory of Trevor Alison
to Librarian Marilyn Thompson for use in the library.
A collection was made in memory of Mr Alison - Head of English -
after he died in a road accident on April 28th 1998.

CHAPTER 13

JULIAN CHARTRES, 1998-2000

Julian Chartres joined the Bemrose Staff from Sarson High School, Melton Mowbray where he had been Acting Head during a period of great uncertainty; when the future of that school lay in the balance. Ironically, his move to Derby brought him to a very similar position, and within a short time of joining the Authority he faced an identical situation in a school fighting for survival.

When he became Head Teacher the School was facing the problem of falling rolls, the number of pupils having fallen from 720 to just over 600. No one appeared to want their children to attend Bemrose School. Fewer pupils resulted in less income to run the school. The management team had been slimmed down at the suggestion of the Ofsted Inspectors who considered it to be top heavy.

It was much to his credit that Julian Chartres (known to all as JC) never lost his sense of humour throughout the problems he faced. However, his dry and often cutting sense of the ridiculous did not appeal to all. His acerbic wit was not universally appreciated or understood by many. The Staff, it is said, would often emerge looking quite bemused after the morning briefing had concentrated on the rivalries of the local football teams. He was a supporter of Leicester City! He raised a few eyebrows when he arrived at school in tight fitting black leather bikers' gear on a magnificent bright red motor cycle.

The need for funding led him to consider a range of initiatives, and the eventual proposal that the school should apply for Enhanced Resource Status for children with communication difficulties was received with very mixed feelings. Inevitably, there seemed to be little alternative and the unit was established on the school balcony. Even that decision was controversial as it involved removing the organ. The instrument which had been such a pride and joy to the Old Bemrosians who had worked so hard to fund it was consigned to the scrap heap.

By this time, the school served pupils aged 11 to 16, but other schools were starting to re-establish their sixth forms. Bemrose School had decided that they would continue with the policy of the Local Education Authority, with pupils moving to sixth form colleges at Mackworth and Normanton. However, to ensure that it could match the facilities offered by competing schools, a range of Post 16 courses was offered. Together with the neighbouring Littleover and Derby Moor Schools these were known as the Millennium Centre. GNVQs were offered in Business, Travel and Tourism, Health and Social Care, ICT and Art and Design. The former music rooms were redeveloped into a Sixth form base, which meant that the music room was moved into the Technology block.

The towers dominate the skyline
Photo courtesy Andy Savage www.derbyphotos.co.uk

One very unusual source of extra income was the use of the school for a Children's Television series called "Whizziwig". There were visits from the crew with enormous trailers of equipment, vans with the actors, and electric cables all over the school. Quite a few of the pupils became "extras" in the series, and not surprisingly the media became a popular career ambition for pupils. The catering van was very popular with staff who turned up at school during the holiday. Maurice Turner, the caretaker, was ensured a hearty breakfast after turning up so early for the filming.

This insight into the media was extended when a team from Bemrose Community School featured in Channel 4's "Big Breakfast" programme. This was not quite on a par with "Top of the Form" from the 1950's!

Chartres initiated a very professional glossy brochure to promote the School and its attractive building. Bemrose School was moving with the times, and aggressive marketing was one strategy in a very competitive area. "Achieving Together" had a strong mission statement of encouragement to all pupils to attain the highest level of achievement of which they were capable, and irrespective of ability, they were encouraged to reach their true potential. Ironic that this was one of the primary wishes for the School back in 1930.

The printing company Bemrose UK had always had close ties with the school. There was a representative of the Company on the School

Governing Body. A broadsheet for the Local Community living in the area around the school, *Bemrose and Community* was published for an 11 year period, but their own financial difficulties, together with constant problems with meeting the publishing deadlines, resulted in their withdrawal of support after 46 issues. There is little contact with the famous publishing company any more.

In October 1998 the school was revisited by the Ofsted team to evaluate progress on the implementation of the Bemrose Community School Action Plan after the 1996 inspection. Julian Chartres was praised for his strong leadership and clear sense of direction. The

Pictures from the School Brochure (above right)
include the Library (above) and cookery class (left)

147

efforts to improve the ethos and develop a work ethic amongst the pupils in a more purposeful learning environment were acknowledged. A clearer focus on raising attainment and improving the atmosphere in the classroom was recognised. However, the Head and Senior Management Team continued to attend *Improve the Quality of Education for All* (IQEA) courses at Nottingham University, whilst Middle Management was trained to accept increased accountability for improved teaching, target setting, mentoring and tracking pupil progress.

A two week timetable was introduced, to enable all subjects to be covered on a repeating cycle - and this concept of 'Week One' and 'Week Two' is still in use, much to the confusion of many.

Despite all efforts, numbers continued to fall and the reputation of the school was called into question. By January 2000 there were rumours that a Secondary School in Derby may be closed. There were too many surplus places in Derby schools and the local authority faced the prospect of withdrawal of Government support unless the problem was tackled. Consultation meetings with the Local Education Authority involved Sinfin School, Village School and Bemrose School. Other schools had managed to reduce their "surplus" in other ways.

One proposal was to create a super school, combining all three schools on one site. This was considered to be a popular concept with the Government, creating a fresh start under a new name. Alternatives included the closing of one of the schools and then combining their numbers with the remaining establishments.

The Consultation Meetings were bitter and acrimonious. Some suspected the LEA of a hidden agenda suggesting that the meetings were a sham and that the decision had already been made in closed circles. During the 15 months of consultation and speculation there remained much uncertainty at all three schools, profoundly affecting staff morale and disruption for the pupils. Long-term damage was inevitable. Parents considered it unwise to send their children to a school which might be closed and their children unable to complete their full five year education. They voted with their feet! Many staff decided to move for more secure jobs and it proved almost impossible to secure replacements. Many supply teachers and temporary teachers were employed to plug the gaps.

Public Meetings were very heated. Head of Lifelong Learning, Councillor Hardyl Dhinsda and Director of Education, Andrew Flack faced hostile questions. Top Management were at greatest risk. Closure of their school would leave them with no school to manage. They would not be offered alternative employment like many of their junior colleagues. Not surprisingly, the Head of Bemrose School, Julian Chartres, was amongst the many who began to look elsewhere. A headship with a more secure future, with the opportunity to plan ahead was what he had thought was on offer when he joined the school.

In 2000 he accepted the headship of Ernesford Grange Community School in Coventry. When it was finally announced in April 2001, that the school which would close was to be Village School, and its 500 pupils be integrated into Bemrose or Sinfin, Julian Chartres was already in post elsewhere. £3.1 million was granted by the Government to create new facilities at the receiving schools.

Sandra Fletcher, the Deputy Head, became acting Head Teacher facing an enormous task. After the first attempt to secure a replacement Head Teacher failed Sandra battled on for 12 months before the post was filled.

The Mayor, Sarah Bolton presents prizes on World Book Day, with Julian Chartres (head) and Miss Janet Snowden (English Teacher)

World Book Day Julian Chartres with Becky Green (Head of English)

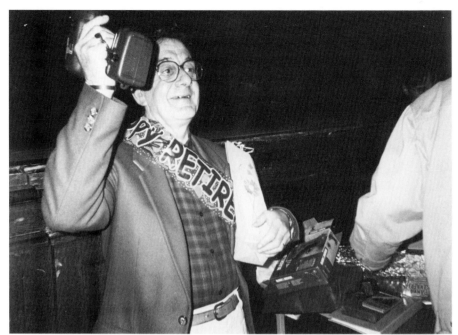

Caretaker Maurice Turner at his retirement presentation January 31st 2001

The paved court yard

Photo courtesy Andy Savage www.derbyphotos.co.uk

CHAPTER 14

RICHARD FEIST, 2001-2003

Richard Feist, B.Com, M.Ed, formerly Head of Aldercar School, Langley Mill, Derbyshire and then Head of Holgate School, Barnsley was appointed Head in

September 2001. At the first attempt, a candidate of the required calibre could not be found, leading to the Governing Body offering an enhanced salary to entice other applicants. Richard Feist was considered by far the best candidate in every respect.

He was welcomed as the dynamic Head who was to "turn the school around". He considered it to be his dream appointment and was sure that he had the skills to help the school to become happy and successful. He hoped to preside over the rise of talent both within the existing Staff and from new appointments.

When he arrived, it was against a background of falling rolls and diminishing reputation. The association in people's minds, and constant comparison to the old Grammar School days had created an impression of a troubled school, with low staff morale and serious weaknesses.

His immediate priority was to alter the School's image and tackle the underlying problems in order to make it a successful school in a multicultural environment. He put the students first, consulted them at all times, listened to their ideas, and acted on their suggestions. Even during his interview for the job, he spent a great deal of time talking to the students, trying to ascertain their hopes and aspirations for the School and for themselves. His style of headship could be summed up as one of maximum daily contact and communication with parents, teachers and students. He followed his own rule, and his techniques gave the Staff ground for much hope for the future.

On many an occasion the staff would be waiting for him to arrive at morning briefings, when he had been delayed by students in the corridors and class rooms en route. He would never brush them away, always listen.

At his first ever full staff meeting, he stunned everyone by criticising their negativity. It was the staff who were at fault not the students. They had a duty to work with the Students and the materials we were given. "The loyalty, support, understanding and kindness received from everyone, totally belied the public perception of a school of no-hopers who had lost the plot".

BEMROSE COMMUNITY SCHOOL — Uttoxeter New Road, Derby, DE22 3HU, TEL: 01332 366711, FAX: 01332 296955, Email: admin@bemrose.derby.sch.uk

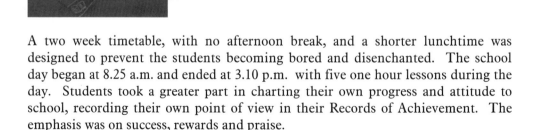

The introduction of a new logo and a completely new uniform, designed by the students themselves, in totally different colours, gave the pupils an identity. Throughout the School, the new colours of blue and purple were used for books, stationery and even the decoration of the walls and ceilings. A new logo, an open book, replaced the "buck" from the park. The house system was re-introduced with the names the famous country houses of Derbyshire: Kedleston, Hardwick, Haddon and Chatsworth replacing the "famous" men from history. Registration took place in house groups, although the lessons continued in year groups as before.

A two week timetable, with no afternoon break, and a shorter lunchtime was designed to prevent the students becoming bored and disenchanted. The school day began at 8.25 a.m. and ended at 3.10 p.m. with five one hour lessons during the day. Students took a greater part in charting their own progress and attitude to school, recording their own point of view in their Records of Achievement. The emphasis was on success, rewards and praise.

Regular uniform checks and a "Best Start" arrangement were introduced. Assertive discipline was established throughout the school. This was no fancy new fangled policy, but was one way to ensure that everyone understood exactly what to expect whether for good or bad behaviour so that a consistent approach was encouraged. Truancy and lateness were identified and tackled, almost immediately, through the newly installed BROMCOM electronic registration system. Punishments included a Head Master's detention.

The withdrawal room was made less welcoming. With no "skive dens", no leaving the School at lunchtime without written permission, and several "out of bounds" areas, the front of the School and the Administration Area became no-go areas for students.

The Student Council was revived, allowing the Students an input to govern their own School. The Parent Teacher Association has been revived.

Despite the many changes introduced, Mr Feist felt that the School was never properly understood by the Local Education Authority or the Government. They appeared to believe that problems could be solved by resources over and above the norm.

Construction work begins on a controversial £1.7m extension in 2002
Photo courtesy Andy Savage www.derbyphotos.co.uk

In 2002, a £1.7M building development and refurbishment programme enhanced facilities. It offered five networked PC laboratories, six refurbished science laboratories, specialist dance/drama studio and new multi-gym. The rebuilding also

Photo courtesy Andy Savage www.derbyphotos.co.uk

included a new visitor entrance in the area once utilized by the library, and before that the Refectory. The reduction in the size of the Library accommodated a waiting area for visitors, fully staffed reception area, disabled access and a lift.

The decision caused controversy as the architectural lines of the School were despoiled by the joining up of the front of the School's open quadrangle. Campaigners tried to stop the building works, assuming that the building was a graded listed building, but that proved to be incorrect and the elegance of the style was sacrificed in favour of more practical issues. The new block was seen as an insensitive addition, and two Old Bemrosians, both now distinguished architects, applied through the Civic Society to the Department of Media, Culture and Sport to have the building spot-listed. However, English Heritage recommended the application be refused on the grounds of insufficient national importance as an inter-war purpose built Grammar School, of which a good few survive.

When the new building was commissioned security was a major concern, and a complex system of key coded entrance doors, together with a sophisticated CCTV system was installed.

A new fundamental problem arose from the LEA's unavoidable policy of filling the empty school places created by obvious social drift from the city to the suburbs which could not be resolved by money alone. Over a quarter of the students needed intensive help to get back on track. The problem was alleviated by employing more teaching assistants and non-teaching Staff who could deal with the students on a one to one basis thus improving the overall school performance.

There were new units for learning support, and for pupils at risk of exclusion from school. There was an enhanced resource facility for those with particular problems. The EAL unit provided for the many students from other cultures whose first language was not English

Gifted and talented pupils were not forgotten either, with a mentor to encourage their development and progress.

Richard disliked the National Curriculum, especially at Key Stage 3. He claimed it was "middle-class, rigid, passive, wordy, irrelevant and non-experimental"! Harsh words, but met with much relief when the complete revamp of the Key Stage 4 Curriculum occurred during his Headship.

He noted that all that links the modern Bemrose to the original founded in 1930 is the basic building, the name and the purpose. That both have, and should have strived for the highest quality of education given the social context in which both operated should never be doubted. To judge either by the prevailing cultural values and context that prevailed for the other was crass. He continued "My most fervent wish for the future is that the school never again fails to move on, retaining from its past only that which is worthy, honourable and relevant to the students". They have always to come first, as generations of talented and committed members of Bemrose School.

The numbers had fallen from 814 pupils in January 2001 to 708 pupils in January 2002, and the school remained unpopular and undersubscribed. The introduction of parental preference had led people to vote with their feet. They felt that the School wasn't providing the education that was required.

Richard Feist was praised for his "very good leadership" and his efforts to improve the School. Ofsted stated that the School is very well led and managed, providing clear direction which has been instrumental in bringing about change subsequent to a period of turbulence and uncertainty. A programme of change, to reach the required standards involved new systems and procedures in teaching and mentoring had resulted in a better learning environment that inspired pupils to be more confident and a desire to do well. Standards of work were improved in Maths, Music, Geography and Information Technology.

Parents and carers viewed the school as very approachable, handling concerns well and with sensitivity. There was promotion of racial harmony and understanding. Real progress was being made, attendance and punctuality improved. Relationships were better, between staff, students, parents, governors and the community. The School helped the pupils to become more mature.

Richard Feist's arrival had been heralded with much promise, and his vision for the school was praised on many occasions. However, as he gradually lost the power to walk and talk, by the start of 2002 he knew his illness was serious and that his dream future was not to be. The onset of what had now been diagnosed as Motor Neurone Disease was cruel. Without a serious illness, the task facing him had been enormous, and with it – too much to contemplate. He left in July 2003.

Ofsted was not impressed. After a shaky report in 2002 the School was revisited by HMI in 2003. Shortly after, it was announced that the school was in "Special Measures".

Richard Feist presents the prizes at Year 7 Chatterbox Club

CHAPTER 15

Ms JOANNE WARD AND THE FUTURE

Joanne Ward became Head Teacher of Bemrose Community School from Easter 2004. She holds a BSc degree in Mathematics and an MA in Education. She moved from Nether Stowe High School in Lichfield – an 11-18 Comprehensive School of 962 pupils.

Her Majesty's Inspectors of Schools had identified serious weaknesses in the quality of education in their report of September 2002. Sandra Fletcher became Acting Head whilst the school awaited a New Head, and she negotiated with the Inspectors in March 2003 when they returned to assess the progress made since the Report of September 2002.

Bemrose Community School failed the inspection and so Ms Ward arrived to face a school in "Special Measures".

When the School was placed in "Special Measures" the Local Authority supported and advised the School and its Governing Body.

A new Assistant Head was appointed to tackle the problems, raise pupil attainment and improve punctuality and attendance. He introduced an early intervention system for absences, together with a system of rewards with credits for attendance and punctuality.

Teaching and learning were closely monitored. Target setting days and progress tests were initiated in all subjects. Gold, silver and bronze learner status, according to the level of achievement, was introduced. Benchmarking and tracking student performance revealed promising signs of improving attainment at Key Stages 3 and 4.

Various other strategies included mentors and pupil involvement through a Student Council. Elected members of each year group believe strongly in the School and have a fervent desire for it to do well. One full-time teacher and seven teaching assistants work with small groups of students in curriculum support. There is an attendance team with an Education Welfare Officer, youth workers and teaching staff and the Learning Support Unit works with students with emotional and behavioural difficulties.

Parents' evenings are now better attended, rising from 35% to 60% support.

The level of turbulence in the School is well above the national average. There continues to be a transient population in the school, with 140 pupils coming and going mid term between September and December 2003. The School has pupils who speak 46 different languages.

Sandra Fletcher was singled out as the main catalyst for change when after 15 months the School emerged from the doldrums in record time. This was held to be against the odds especially when the "turbulence" was considered.

So What of the Future?

The partnership between the new Head Teacher Jo Ward and Mrs Fletcher as Associate Head has continued, quite a change for Bemrose School to have two female leaders.

As a school, Bemrose is well resourced and financially sound. All teachers have laptop computers and each area has interactive whiteboards and projectors. There are five IT suites.

Should the School consider Specialist College Status? Most Secondary Schools in Derby and Derbyshire are now Technology Colleges, or Centres of Excellence in Languages, Performing Arts, Engineering, Science, Sports or Maths and Computing.

More recently, there were rumours that Bemrose School may become a City Academy, run by businesses with £25million donated by the Government and £2 million by the Sponsor. Academies were established in 2001 in disadvantaged areas of low educational standards. They are much favoured by the Government, but would be outside the control of the Local Authority, so the concept is strongly opposed by the Governors of the School.

The Curriculum now provides more relevant opportunities for many pupils through vocational courses. There is a sixth form, in liaison with two other schools, providing good opportunities for a small group of students. Will the International Baccalaureate Diploma - a two year pre-university course and examination be a way forward?

Currently, 800 Students are organised into four houses with six or seven mixed year groups in each house.

Students represent a wide range of ethnic groupings with 46% white, 7% black, 31% Pakistani and 3% Indian. They come from some of the poorest areas in Derby with 47% having English as an additional language and 41% having free school meals. 41% have special educational needs.

The school has an excellent Inclusion and Language Support Unit, together with an Enhanced Resource Facility for children with communication difficulties.

A new innovation, the first of its kind in the country, has been the appointment of a member of the police force to talk to younger Students about the role and powers of the Police, and to older pupils about personal safety issues. The project has been financed by Derby Community Safety Partnership and supported by Derby Homes. A principal object is the improvement of attendance among older pupils.

The school is a designated training School in the East Midlands Training Schools Consortium, helping students to progress their careers and providing a quality support and training opportunity to the School Staff. A specialist I.T. coach has been added to the team, as part of the I.C.T. and Mobility Project.

Bemrose has the benefit of a range of additional funding including Excellence in Cities and Leadership Incentive Grant funding. There has been a successful bid to Creative Partnerships and to LSC for South Derby Consortium.

Many innovations are being considered, including the continuous teaching day and use of Datapower for in School monitoring of targets.

Bemrose has gained several awards including Health Promoting Schools Award, Diana Princess of Wales Memorial Award, Partnership Promotion and Success through Learning, and the Basic Skills Quality Mark.

The School looks forward with confidence as it lives up to its mission to be a welcoming School for all abilities and ethnic groups. Most of all it continues to meet the objectives made for the School on the opening day back in 1930 albeit in very different circumstances.

On Thurs 26th March 2009 Bemrose School took part in the BBC News School Report project. The students were asked to report on topical, national and regional news and present it in a variety of ways including written, audio and video reports.

160

*The Clock Tower
and Foundation
Stone*

*Below, this area is
now enclosed by the
New Building which
joins up the former
Quadrangle*

*Photos courtesy
Andy Savage
www.derbyphotos.co.uk*

*The new Community/Dining Hall is on the left and the new Design and Technology Block
is in the centre of this picture*

View of the School from Uttoxeter New Road

Photos courtesy Andy Savage www.derbyphotos.co.uk

APPENDICES

APPENDIX 1

SOME OLD BEMROSIANS OF DISTINCTION

Many Old Bemrosians enjoyed successful careers. They made the grade in all walks of life, and many left their mark with notable contributions to the nation. The school has reason to be proud that it fostered so many successful careers.

The list is far from being a complete record and only provides examples. Apologies to the many not included.

ACADEMICS

ALAN BREWER: Oriel College, Oxford, Lecturer in Meteorology. F.R.S. 1946. Delivered Bakerian Lecture on water content of the stratosphere.

GEORGE DIXON: Awarded the Mercator Prize in Geography at Birmingham University 1949. Most distinguished student in final year examinations.

PHILIP FREEMAN: Commonwealth Fellow in Architecture.

W F HALL: Principal of Secondary School in Salisbury, Rhodesia, St. Mary's Mission, Hunyani.

JOHN MANSFIELD: Geologist and Geophysicist on RSS Shackleton in British Antarctica.

ROBERT MATTHEWS: Chartered Physicist, Fellow of the Royal Astronomical Society, Fellow of the Royal Statistical Society. Science correspondent in The Sunday Telegraph, Focus, World Link and Four Four Two.

SYDNEY MUSGROVE: Professor. English Language and Literature Development, Auckland University, New Zealand. Elizabethan Stage Production. Carnegie Grant for Drama and Adult Education.

FREDERICK SAMUEL NORTHEDGE: Professor in International Relations, Carnegie Endowment of International Peace, Author of 14 books.

JOHN NORMAN SMITH: Senior Lecturer in Chemistry, University of Dunedin, New Zealand.

JOHN SYDNEY SUTTON: CBE 1966. Education Consultant. Director, International Business Education Co-operation Charitable Trust. General Secretary of the Secondary Heads Association. Former Teacher and Head of History at Bemrose School.

KENNETH VARTY: Professor Medieval, Renaissance Studies, and French Literature.

ARTS, MUSIC, DRAMA AND LITERATURE

JAMES BOLAM: Actor. Attended the Central School of Speech and Drama in London where he was awarded a Gold Medal, gained the Margaret Rawlings Trophy for Diction, and the Elsie Fogarty Prize for Best All Round Performance by a Man. Born in Sunderland in 1938. Regularly appears on television. Appeared in The Likely Lads, When the Boat Comes In, Only when I Laugh, Beiderbecke and continues in many today.

JOHN K BRIERLEY: Wrote two books about his father Walter Brierley who wrote "The Means Test Man" about life on the dole in the 1930's. John Brierley served as an Intelligence Officer with the Sherwood Foresters before gaining a doctorate at Queen's College Oxford. He was visiting Fellow at Merton College, Oxford and eventually became an Inspector of Schools.

ROB CHILDS: Children's author, writing a very popular series of more than 50 books about Football and Cricket. "The Big Match" series and "Time Rangers" are published by Corgi Books. Works with Dyslexic Students to help them overcome their difficulties.

RALPH W. DOWNES: Organist and choral conductor. Designed the organ installed at the Royal Festival Hall in 1951. Fellow of the Royal College of Music. Assistant Organist at Southwark Cathedral 1923. Organist at Brompton Oratory 1936-1977.

TREVOR EAST: Disc Jockey and Local Media Personality. He became Head of Sport at ITV and was accredited with the decision by Des Lynam to move from the BBC and join ITV. A presenter of the Saturday morning slapstick entertainment "Tiswas" with Chris Tarrant.

ALWYN EDGAR: Book publisher Alston Books, concentrated on history, children's books, biography, current affairs and education. Produced "The Flight to Varennes".

REG FLETCHER: Assistant conductor of Winchester Festival Choir, enjoyed a successful career as a professional singer and conductor before becoming a teacher. Music adviser and inspector in Hampshire and Ofsted inspector.

KENNETH IVAN FORD: Methodist Minister. Youngest ever ordinand at the time (?1939) of the Birmingham Methodist College. Used to "preach" in the school yard at lunchtime 1934 – 36. Last charge Portland, Dorset 1992. Patrol Leader 55th Group which won Drury-Lowe Camping Trophy 1934.

TOM HENRY: Managing Editor, Manchester Evening News.

MICHAEL KNOWLES: Actor. Attended RADA. Starred in "It Ain't Half Hot Mum", "Dad's Army" and "Hi De Hi". *See photograph and information in the Bennett era.*

ERIC LANDER: Television Actor in the crime series "Lockhart" and "No Hiding Place". Shakespeare productions at Stratford. Films included "The Colditz Story" and "Sink the Bismarck". Top Drama Producer of "The White Falcon", "Sexton Blake", "Coronation Street" 1972-74, "The Business of Murder" 1983-86 at Mayfair Theatre.

ADRIAN LEE: Conductor and Instrumentalist.

KEVIN REARDON LLOYD: Actor on stage, radio and television. Member of the Bristol Old Vic and Royal Shakespeare Company. Television roles in "Z Cars", "Coronation Street", "Auf Wiedersehen Pet" and "Minder". Over 400 appearances in ITV's "The Bill" as Tosh Lines. Died 1998.

TERENCE (Terry) ELLIS LLOYD: Television journalist, well known for his reporting from the Middle East. Terry made tragic headlines himself when he was killed on March 22nd, 2003 in Iraq while covering the 2003 invasion of Iraq for ITN.

TONY 'NAT' LOFTAS: Author of "The Wealth of the Ocean" and "The Last Resource", then switched to journalism as editor of "Discovery", "Hydrospace" and the science section of "Science Journal".

CHRISTOPHER LYNDON-GEE: Composer and Conductor. Saarbrucken Radio Symphony Orchestra.

IAN MORSON: Crime writer, short stories, mystery novels and book reviews.

ANTON RIPPON: Book Publisher, Breedon Books, specializing in Derby and Derbyshire. Columnist in Derby Telegraph. Writes on Derby County F.C.

DON SHAW: Playwright, actor, teacher and novelist. Recently wrote "The Hike" about the Derbyshire Peak District. Wrote many TV and radio dramas including "Dangerfield", "Beyond Fear", "A Question of Honour" and "Me Mackenzie", "The Giants". LRAM Speech and Drama 1967. Taught at schools in Derby. Performed at Derby Playhouse, Derby Shakespeare Society and Derby Theatre in the Round. Radio, storytelling, talks, drama and religious broadcasts.

JOHN STRAW: Professional Artist, painting wildlife and landscapes. Commercial illustrator including calendars, greetings cards and magazine covers. Regular exhibitions of his work.

BUSINESS AND INDUSTRY

ALAN ATKIN: Manager, Barclays Bank, Burton on Trent.

LEWIS R BEESLEY: Director of Engine Production, Ministry of Supply.

PETER BREWIN: Director Bemrose and Sons.

PETER COLSTON: Director of Aero Engine Division, Rolls Royce. Despite failing his 11 plus, and later contracting polio at Manchester University, Peter had a meteoric career; rising from an apprentice in the Rolls Royce Purchasing Department to taking charge of their £150 million a year budget. He spent 10 months in a wheelchair after becoming paralysed in the left arm and the diaphragm, but continued at work after being told he was unemployable "no firm would want to employ a cripple". Later suffered a heart attack in 1973 but returned to work after 12 weeks. An example of triumph over adversity. Patriotic Service Award, Bishops Industrial Council.

BRIAN COXON: Group Managing Director, Maxwell Data Management, Chairman of Derby Playhouse.

GORDON R DOLEMAN: Managing Director Bristol Engine Division, Rolls Royce.

GEOFFREY HORTON: Section Manager, Rolls Royce.

W V GREATOREX: Distinguished Flying Cross, Captain with British European Airways.

NIGEL RUDD: Left Bemrose School aged 16 to train as an Accountant. Purchased Williams & Sons (later called Williams Holdings) in 1980s. Chairman of Pilkington 1994. Chairman of Boots from 2003. Non-executive Chairman of Kidde. Chairman of Barclays plc. Chairman of Derby Pride. Deputy Lord Lieutenant of Derbyshire. Knighted in 1996.

STANLEY W TACEY: Manager, Composing Room, Bemrose Printers. Vice President Derbyshire County Cricket Club, Scorer 1995 – 2000.

F J WALKER: Assistant Controller of one of the Big Five banks.

JEFF R WHEATLEY: Managing Director of the 600 Group of Companies.

DEREK YOUNG: Leverhulme Prize for Proficiency in Cost Accountancy 1960.

V R W YOUNG: Chairman of Birmingham Institute of Management Personnel.

MEDICAL, LEGAL AND ADMINISTRATIVE PROFESSIONS

DOUGLAS RODNEY ALLEN: Shipping Manager Rolls Royce, Import/Export Services East Midlands Airport, Methodist Minister 1987 serving Erewash Valley, Ashby and Coalville Circuits.

CHARLES BALDWIN: Professor of Oncology.

PHIL BEDFORD: Specialised in Oncology.

MICHAEL BLETCHER: Derby's Police Surgeon. Medical adviser and inspiration behind the Dangerfield series by Don Shaw.

KEITH CARTER: Member of the Royal College of Surgeons at the age of 22, 1949.

R A M GREGSON: PhD 1961. Experimental Psychology on Human Food Preferences.

F T HUNT: Medical Officer for the County Borough of Derby, then Medical Officer of Health for Totnes.

BRIAN LUX: Member of the General Dental Council and writer of magazine articles and books.

JOSEPH MARKLAND: County Analyst for Derbyshire. Fellow of the Royal Institute of Chemistry 1946.

CHARLES GREATOREX: Physicist, Royal Cancer Establishment, Sutton.

J A HICKLIN: Buxton and Letheby Prizes for Scholarship in Physiology, London Hospital.

DENNIS HINCKLEY: Police Cadet, HM Forces with 6th Airborne Division in France, Germany and Italy, present at Luneberg Heath in 1945 when hostilities formally ended. Rejoined the Police in administration. Finance Officer to Derbyshire Fire Service

MARK JELLEY: Outstanding career is Psychology and Gynaecology

STANLEY B MARSH: Doctor, Head of Law, Manchester Polytechnic College of Commerce.

HUGH PRICE: General Practitioner, Park Lane Surgery, Allestree, Derby. Derby Shakespeare Society. Talented Amateur Cricketer.

JOHN READ: Doctor specialising in treatment of Cancer by Radium, awarded David Anderson Berry Prize as the man who has done most for the human race in the 1930's.

R L TRAVIS: Preston Prize and Medal for Distinction in Operative Dentistry, Manchester 1949.

JOHN L WEBB: Chief Legal Officer, Rolls Royce. Secretary of the Aero Engine Division.

POLITICS & CIVIL SERVICE

DAVID BLACK: Formerly Conservative Councillor for Spondon, Derby. Currently Chairman of Derby UK Independence Party.

DAVID FLETCHER: Councillor Newcastle under Lyme and East Staffordshire 1957-1995.

E R FOX: Parliamentary Commentator at BBC Sound and Television.

GEORGE EMERY: Principal Executive Officer Ministry of Fuel and Power, Ministry of Supply, Ministry of Aviation, Ministry of Technology 1967, Knighted CB in 1980, Director General of Defence Accounts, Ministry of Defence 1973-1980.

ROYDEN GREENE: J.P., Councillor, Chair of Governors at Bemrose School, Conservative Parliamentary Candidate for South Derby.

J B JOHNSTON: Her Majesty's High Commissioner in Southern Rhodesia. Knighted 1966 Commander of the Order of St. Michael and St. George.

D J KING: Deputy High Commissioner for Penang and North Malaysia.

J S H (Josh) WHITE: Senior Civil Servant

QUIZ SHOW CONTESTANTS

GORDON TUNNICLIFFE: Participant in the 64 Thousand Dollar Question 1991, Specialist subject "The Canals of England".

ERIC SAUNDERS: One of the first winners of BBC TV Mastermind.

SCIENCE & ENGINEERING

RICHARD E. ALLSOP: O.B.E. 1997 for Services to Traffic Management and Road Safety, Highways and Transportation, Award for Professional Distinction 1997, Professor of Transport Studies at University College, London. 170 articles in publications on Road Safety.

STEWART ANDERSON: Chairman and Chief Executive, British Waterways. Knighted.

SIDNEY ALFRED BAILEY: Mechanical Engineer, awarded Herbert Akroyd Stuart Prize on Dynamic Absorber Crankshafts. 1942.

S C BREARLEY: Awarded the Perry Medal for Mathematics and Mechanics, Imperial College of Science, 1941.

A W DAVIES: President of Derby Society of Engineers.

RICHARD A DODD: Awarded Doctorate by Birmingham University for his research work on Industrial Metallurgy.

DOMLEO: Grandson of Herbert Spencer Domleo who was the Mayor of Derby. Senior Railway Engineer, South Australian Transport. Australian National Railway, Australia Rail and Track Ltd. Worked on the Channel Tunnel.

E G ECCLESHARE: Senior Industrial Gas Engineer.

RAYMOND G FLOWER: Master Engineer (R.A.F. Command) on the Comet flying the Prime Minister to the Washington Conference in 1960.

ALAN FREDERICK GIFFORD: Chief Welding Engineer at International Combustion Limited, working on power stations world wide. Chairman of the East Midlands Branch of the Welding Institute. Furthered the development of Argon welding. Rode in the Brighton to Glasgow Cycle Race in 1952. Wrote book on Derbyshire Windmills.

BILL GOODCHILD: Built a one third replica model of Captain James Cook's Historic Ship "Endeavour" as a tourist attraction, beached in Caloundra, Queensland, Australia.

ROY HARTLE: Head of a team of Specialist Engineers responsible for data collection at British Rail Research.

KENNETH SOAR HOLMES: Brigadier, Telephone Engineer of great distinction.

DONALD T SARFAS: Chartered Chemist, R & D Chemist ICI. Fellow Royal Society of Chemistry. Staff Tutor Amateur Swimming Association. Life Member Manchester & District Swimming and Water Polo Association.

DEREK TERRY: Member of Geological Expedition to North Spitzgergen, Arctic, maintaining mechanical equipment.

P A WEBSTER: Pye Communications, Member of British Institution of Radio Engineers, working on Jodrell Bank experiments reflecting radio waves off the moon.

SERVICES

J G BROOKES: Lieut. Commander, MBE.

DEREK HASLEM BUCKLEY: Corporal RAF, Enigma Code Breaker at Bletchley Park during World War 2. Later Reverend Canon.

PETER DAVIES: Lieutenant, M.C. for services in Razmac, India.

NIGEL PETER EMPSON: Best All Round Apprentice, HMS Collingwood.

KENNETH S HOLMES: Director of Army Postal Services.

CLIVE MILNER: Armoured Corps of the Canadian Army. Commandant at Land Forces Command and Staff College. Officer of the Order of Military Merit. Awarded Meritorious Service Cross.

ANTHONY L SLADE: Accounts Clerk, RAF Coningsby. Served in Aden, Cyprus and Kenya.

TIMOTHY SMITH: Sergeant in the British Army, BEM 1989.

WILLIAM LOGAN SOWTER: Fighter and Bomber Pilot, WW2, Bombers. Air Force Cross.

SPORT AND GAMES

M BASSANO: Under 21 Team, World Sabre Championships.

 JAMES HERBERT BEETHAM: World Billiard Champion in 1960. English Amateur Billiards Champion in 1966 and 1968. Director of White Bros (Derby) Ltd, soft drink manufacturers.

MARTIN BENNEY: Represented Great Britain at Swimming.

SYDNEY BRADLEY: Chairman, Derby County FC.

ANDREW BURTON: English Schools Basketball Team.

SIMON GILMORE, RAY GAMBLE AND MAURICE HILL: County Chess Champions. In 1962 the School was awarded a shield for outstanding achievement in chess by the British Chess Federation.

DAVID HAYNES: England Basketball Team.

COLIN MORTLOCK (*right*): Led a six-man kayak expedition along the Arctic coastline of Norway and round the North Cape. This was followed by two-man and solo expeditions

STEVE POWELL (*left*): Captain of English Schoolboys Football Team. Debut for Derby County in 1971 aged 16, after selection by Brian Clough. Right back, but played in most positions, 22 league games in 1971-2, 29 in 1972-3, played in European Cup and in a second championship in 1974-5 when still only 19. Injury ended his football career.

TOMMY POWELL (*right*): Father of Steve Powell. Signed for Derby County in 1942, he played over 400 games for the Rams, retiring in 1962.

CHRIS RIGGOTT: Derby County defender, later moved to Middlesbrough.

KEITH STEVENSON: Chairman of Derbyshire Cricket Club.

MAURICE WOODMANSEE: 1990 Australian Croquet Champion and played at interstate level.

BEMROSE SCHOOL
LIST OF STAFF

Several hundred members of staff have been employed during the last 75 years. Many are remembered with great affection and gratitude; others left a legacy of fear. Some are described as inspirational, caring, dedicated, witty or fun - but others were thought of as unpopular, dour or even cruel.

Career details, qualifications and dates have been acquired from staff records – but the real descriptions come from the anecdotes and abiding memories of their pupils.

John Dominy from Aston on Trent wrote:
"Teachers dedicated to their profession and the welfare and training of their pupils must have spent hours marking homework or class work, giving extra tuition and help to pupils and preparing visual aids for use in class. Above all they taught discipline and self discipline. They knew how to punish in all sorts of ways, some of which could be momentarily painful and would be a sackable offence these days, but the boys accepted it all in the knowledge that it was deserved and later on in life came to realise that it was all part of training for adult life."

THE TEACHERS ARE LISTED IN ALPHABETICAL ORDER OF THEIR SURNAME.
If there is a letter after the entry and the surname is in bold type - you may find more information in the chapter on the relevant era - **M** for Macfarlane, **B** Bennett, **C** Chapman, **W** Wearne, **H** Hobson, **K** Kenney, **JC** Chartres and **F** Feist

Do you remember?......

"Pop" **ALLEN** taught maths and geography. Later became Head Teacher of Brighton Road School, Derby, 1945. An ex-naval man, he walked about his geography room as if on the bridge of a ship, bearded, narrow faced and weather beaten. Kind and interesting he suffered no nonsense. Organised camping holidays at Repton School.

Dave **AMEDRO** nicknamed "Pedro", joined 1959 to teach French, Spanish and Russian. Red faced and bullish, didn't suffer fools gladly.

Ian J **ARNOTT** taught English from 1964-69.

Patsy **ASTLE** taught English, left to become Head of Peartree School, Derby in 1945.

William Tom **BARNETT** BSc Econ, taught at Orchard Street and Brighton Road before joining Bemrose in 1945 to teach geography and economics. Moved to Central School in 1948 and then returned to Bemrose 1950-1971. Owned a Standard Vanguard car. A twinkle in his eye, with a rather formidable exterior. Helped with the Sixth Form Council.

Ivy **BARNSDALL** taught English until 1944. A strict disciplinarian who got results. Acquired a qualification in Hebrew because she wished to study the scriptures in their early form. Moved to St Mary's College, Cheltenham in 1945

Peter "Flap" **BATEMAN. W**

R "Billie" **BAXTER** taught Chemisty from 1920 until he retired in 1953. Gained the Military Cross during WW1, superb cricketer (renowned for his bowling), hockey player and pianist.

E G **BENNETT, HEADMASTER 1951-1957 B**

Michael John "Killer" **BLAKE,** Head of Classics, joined 1930. Retired 1962. **M**

Eric William "Sons" **BRANTHWAITE,** B.A. Liverpool B.Sc. London, taught in Yorkshire, Kendal, Colwyn Bay and Suffolk, before becoming English teacher in 1945 until retirement in 1964.

"Monty" **BREWSTER,** senior lab steward, joined the staff in 1907 and retired in 1947 after 40 years. One of his duties was to shepherd the latecomers who arrived after the registration bell and have them sign the late book. He was great fun, with real goodness of heart and devotion to the interests of the pupils. A cricketer and first aid expert. **M**

A L "Alfy" **BROWN** taught maths from 1929 to 1945 when he moved to become senior maths master at Erith Grammar School. Had a tendency to be sarcastic but funny. Wore a striped yellow and green blazer for refereeing matches. Son of a colliery manager, dark, bespectacled with a Clark Gable moustache. Commanding officer of the school A.T.C. Had a temper, and threw the board rubber around with fair accuracy. His organizing ability was exercised in making out the school timetable and solving crossword puzzles.

"Pobble" **CALVERT** taught maths from 1960.

K A **CAPPS** taught science from 1960-63.

"Mad" Jock T A **CARSON** 1969.

J A "Cuspy" **CARTER** onetime Head of Science, becoming Deputy Head after "Froggy" Freeman, sometimes called "Raich", taught physics for 33 years from 1924 to 1957. Housemaster of Wellington. Timetable organiser from 1930. **M**

Frank A. **CASHIN** 1931 -36. Specially recruited to start German as a subject. Scout Master 1934 – 36. **M**

George **CATTON,** Senior Chemistry master 1947 -55, and died in a road accident 1955. Conscientious man and a good teacher. A devout Christian.

Reverend J E O **CHANDLER,** Head of R.E. from 1965.

Dr W R C **CHAPMAN** "The Cheese", HEADMASTER 1958-1971. **C**

Norman Llewelyn **CLAY,** English teacher from 1931-1933 wrote an English Grammar book and earned a substantial sum in royalties. Needless to say the book was used at Bemrose. Also taught divinity. Moved to Senior English master Eccleshall School.

Paul **CLAYTON**

Arthur Leonard **COOIL,** Mathematics teacher. Responsible for swimming. First joined the staff in 1928 and left in 1945. Returned in 1958 for 4 years and died 1962. Married Margaret Hodge. 2 sons at Bemrose. **M**

Herbert F **COOK,** joined 1948. Taught French. Ginger haired, dynamic man with a high pitched voice. Arranged French pen pals. Promoted to Head of Modern Languages. Considered an outstanding teacher. An inveterate smoker he used to circle errors in the pupils' work with every increasing circles of red ink, with the instruction COR in the margin. **C**

John Anthony **CRAGG** joined 1937 and taught French until 1946.

J "Nobby" **CRITCHLOW** senior Mathematics teacher, joined 1924, left 1958. **M**

Horace **CROSSLEY** teacher of French, joined 1931 and retired in 1950, but was called back because of shortages.

Esmond Emrys Lloyd "Crass" **CROWTHER** joined 1915, retired 1952. Taught History and Latin. **M**

Matthew Brian **CUNNINGHAM** taught Russian and games from 1970. Moved to Christ's Hospital.

F A "Donc" **DAUNCEY,** taught French from 1927 to 1957. **M**

A **DAVIES** taught English from 1958 to 1963, also known as "Peter Wyngarde".

H J **DAVIS** M.A. Oxon. Taught English 1930–34. First Scoutmaster 55th Derby Group. A devout Christian. Appointed Headmaster Whitby Grammar School 1934. **M**

Colin David **DORRELL** German and French teacher from 1957.

Stanley Frederick "Dicky" **DOWNING.** English 1928-1947 produced the Shakespeare plays, moved to become senior English master in Exeter. **M**

J "Charlie" **DUKES**, Chisel Chuckin' Charlie, 1949 – 59.

Kenneth James **EADE** L.R.A.M., A.R.C.M., F.T.C.L. Joined the staff in 1948 and moved to Caterham School, Surrey 1957.**B**

Charles Harold **FITCH,** music teacher from 1930 to 1947, when he moved to Brockenhurst County Grammar School. **M**

M ST J **FORREST** taught classics form 1964.

Thomas Henry "Froggy" **FREEMAN.** Taught French from 1904 until retirement just before WW2. He introduced the school play and also swimming. Born in Halifax he smiled easily and loved to tell a good story. Charming and genial. Took school parties to France, a first class teacher who used phonetics to teach French pronunciation. **M**

Miss **GARDENER** "Flo", taught Latin and ancient Greek. Owned a 1937 "Baby" Austin car.

Paul G "Tiny" **GATLAND,** History and English Teacher from 1964 and Head of General Studies from 1966. Sensitive, thoughtful, a fine historian and excellent cricketer. Left 1969.

Leslie Freeman "Basher" **GENT,** Maths teacher from 1931 to 1944 when he moved to Tynemouth Municipal High School. Not averse to administering a slap at the side of the face if behaviour warranted it.

G L **GIBBS,** a pupil at the school, then a teacher of English from 1966. Acute and perceptive intellect.

Claud Wilson W **GIBSON,** taught French from 1942 to 1949 and a very popular Form Master. Fine athlete and games player, coached football and cricket. Involved in school drama productions. A brilliant teacher, firm but fair.

Eddie **GILDEA.**

Allan **GODDARD** joined 1949

Frank "Thicky" **GOODWIN** joined 1928 as PE teacher, subsequently taught English, French and Geography. Left 1944 for a post at Torquay Grammar School.

D **GRAHAM** taught history 1960-63

Bill **GRAY** of Tyneside origin, joined 1962.

C W **GRIMADELL** "Grim", joined 1952 to teach physics.

D **HABIB** was seldom identified by first name initial. PE particularly fencing. Rumoured to be an Iraqi son of an Eastern potentate. Studied at Loughborough College, reputed to be a champion fencer. Would leave the pupils hanging upside down on the wall bars in the sports hall whilst he read out the notices. Moved to become Chief P.E Adviser to Iraq. Told stories about swimming in the Euphrates, and eating watermelons bought from sellers in boats plying the river.

E Ken **HAND,** joined 1956 to teach art.

Ronald Francis "Ronnie" **HANLON,** pupil from 1929, taught handicrafts from 1940 until he retired in 1978. Married "Fanny" Whetstone biology teacher. **M**

John E "Harry" **HARBACH,** taught physics from 1931, introducing a new brand of physics teaching to a brand new school. Involved with the ATC and the Scientific Society, he was a good teacher with a quiet gentlemanly manner. Retired in 1978.

E V **HARPER,** History Teacher married School Secretary Judith Selby. **B.**

Elizabeth Margery **HAYWARD,** joined 1950, left 1955.

R J **HEATH** taught biology and chemistry from 1964.

George Edgar **HEMMINGS** taught English. Joined 1949 aged 23, left 1958, he was a pupil at the school from 1937-44.

Miss Elsie Eileen **HEPWORTH** "Polly", taught maths from 1935 until retirement in July 1972. Involved in tennis and drama, and also a keen rifle shooter. The school Dramatic Society was a special interest together with the Parents Association and lost property. **M**

Margaret **HIGGINSON**

S **HINDLEY,** became Head of English in 1967.

D N **HOLT,** taught physics from 1960-65

Mary **HOUGH**, French teacher, married Mr Cooil. Firm without being overbearing. Form mistress of 2.3, an avid swimmer, and very well liked. Thought to be camp cook at farm camps.

A HOUSE, "Mickie" or "Bertie", Head of English for 35 years from 1924 to 1959. **M**

S P "Toddy" **HOWELL**, Woodwork teacher for 38 years from 1908 to 1946. **M**

JOHNSON, a former pupil, taught music from 1967.

Olive P **JONES**, "Clarabel" or OP, taught English from 1945 to 1958. Her method for tackling a piece of written work was unique. Producer of the annual school play. Moved to Frome Grammar School, Somerset in 1960 where she was elected to the town council.

Charles J **KITCHELL**, R.E. Teacher and games coach from 1958.

F C "Larry" **LAMB** - BSc Durham, joined 1947 as Assistant Master for General Science and teacher of 6th form biology, left 1955.

Robert Edgar **LISTER**, joined 1934, a pale Liverpudlian biology master. Joined the Royal Signals after his house was bombed. Left 1946 for a post in Gloucester.

Denis **LLOWARCH**, Chemistry teacher from 1933 to 1946, when he moved to St Alban's Grammar School.

Carl Conrad **LOEBER** joined 1949. Held a diploma in P.E. from Loughborough College. Assistant Master P.E., Athletics, games and swimming. Moved to Ernest Bailey Grammar School, Matlock as P.E. Master in 1955.

Harold Gregson "Billy" **LORD**, taught Classics, Ancient History and P.E. from 1930 to 1949. Eccentric, he would read straight from the Greek about the preparation of mummies. Used to punish with a ruler or slipper across the hand, stating that "this hurts me more than it hurts you". A brilliant scholar, he could not control a class of noisy, boisterous younger pupils and moved to become a lecturer at N.W. London Polytechnic.

George Neil **MACDONALD**, joined 1950, educated at St Catherine's College Cambridge and gained a Tripos in Modern and Medieval Languages as well as a BA and then MA. Had been lecturer at the British Institute, Seville, Spain and moved to Stockport School in 1958 to teach Spanish.

W A **MACFARLANE** "The Boss" Headmaster from 1923 to 1951. **See Chapters 4 & 5.**

L **MANCHESTER** taught physics from 1958-61.

Dick **MARRIOTT** taught pure and applied maths from 1957 until his retirement in 1977(?). Became Head of Mathematics in 1963. A meticulous sense of order and great good humour.

J "Jack" **MATHERS** taught mathematics from 1946. He held a 1st class Honours degree (London) and was a man of intellectual distinction and artistic sensitivity. Played bridge. Retired 1972.

Paul Ernest "Monkey" **MAURER** BSc Hons and then MSc, Geography and Latin teacher from 1947 until retirement in 1971. Previously taught in Cheltenham and Surrey prep schools and then in Prague, Yorkshire and Stockport. Rugged and tough, he took charge of Cross-country, rugby and the chess team.

James Roger "Pongo" **MOLYNEUX**, taught French and maths, joined 1945 and retired 1971. Housemaster of Newton.

L J **MORTON** joined 1927, left 1938.

John "Noddy" **NADEN. W**

John **NIXON**, 34 years at Bemrose, teaching mostly Latin and occasionally mathematics from 1908. Sometimes known as honest John, whatever he did, he did well. Housemaster of Sidney. In charge of school football for 20 years, Secretary to the School National Savings Group. He retired early in 1940 because of deafness. He was a keen stamp collector, and judged the Hobbies exhibition stamp collections.

WILLIAM Charles "Nunky" **NORVILL** taught history for 35 years and was also Newton housemaster. Joined 1930, retired 1965. Nicknamed "Umble". **M**

Glencoe Ronald **NUNN** maths and physics teacher from 1957 until retirement in 1964.

ORCHARD taught history from 1960.

Mrs **PACKER** taught scripture, and according to John Brierley in his book, she "stood, big bosomed, like an attractive cow".

Frederick Arthur **PALMER**, joined 1955 and taught chemistry until he retired in 1971.

Mr **PETO**, an Austrian refugee who taught maths.

William Archie "Bill" or "Percy" **PICKERING** taught English for 38 years from 1935 to 1973. **M**

E B **PIERCY,** taught biology from 1960.

Albert Haynes **PIPES,** taught woodwork from 1947. Moved from Mickleover and Hatton Schools until his retirement from Bemrose in 1967.

Dr Arthur Ernest **POPE,** joined 1958 and died aged 40 in 1965. Taught music **B**

W J "Curly" **PRITCHARD,** Teacher of mathematics from 1940 to 1955 when he became a Headmaster in a school in Derby. Red faced and twitchy he was involved in the Bemrose School ATC. Ear tweaking was one of his pastimes on pupils who did not pay attention.

Charles Frederick George **RANSOM,** BSc London, taught geography and economics from 1936 to 1945, when he left after military service and took up a position with the government.

Danny E B **REES**, joined the staff in 1950 to teach P.E. **W**

Brenda Mary **RUFFELL,** taught geography, stood in for her husband during the war.

W R **SAUNDERS**, metalwork teacher from 1949 to 1966. Taught Technical Drawing and Woodwork in the workshop which he built up from its inception. A keen amateur gardener who exhibited at local flower shows.

John E **SCUPHAM**, joined 1934 and left in 1942. English teacher, very strict, would throw chalk at inattentive boys. Quickly lost control. According to John Brierley "he had a crumpled face, sliced by a wide mouth like a kind frog". He loved his subject and transmitted some of its delight to the boys. He achieved a high position in the BBC.

Norman J **ROTHWELL**, also known as "The Blob" or "Big Louie" was Deputy Head and a teacher of history. He was a great believer in corporal punishment, which he administered with relish.

W **SAVIGNY** 1962

Judith **SELBY**, the school secretary and a former beauty queen, married history teacher Mr. Harper.

Maurice "Sammy" **SEVERN**, Geography teacher joined 1946, left 1972, B A Hons from London and also trained P.E. Teacher, taught with enthusiasm bringing geography alive.

P A **SHAW,** another former pupil who joined the maths teaching staff in 1964.

William John Herbert "Joey" **SLATER,** taught geography from 1931 until leaving to teach at Bedales School, Petersfield in 1943.

Major William **SMELLIE,** from 1924 to 1957, taught Latin and Greek. Later Housemaster of Wellington after Mr Carter. Died 1958. **M**

Duncan Charles **SMITH,** taught history and government from 1968 and moved on to become a lecturer at Kesteven College of Education in 1972.

Miss Kate M **SMITH,** from 1918 taught as English teacher and also in charge of the prep school. Left in 1955 after 37 years at Bemrose. **M**

Arthur H "Piggy" **SOWTER,** teacher of French and German. Joined in 1948. B.A. London University took French and modern languages until retirement in 1972.

W S **SPENCER,** taught chemistry for 36 years from 1921 until his retirement in 1957. **M**

John Sydney **SUTTON** taught history from 1960 to 1968. He became head of history in 1965, and moved to a post in Birmingham.

John Malcolm "Jim" **TATE,** was a pupil at the school from 1944-52 and joined the staff in 1958 as chemistry teacher. He moved to Homelands School, Derby in 1970 as Head of Chemistry.

A **TAYLOR** 1965-70

Harold "Squeaky" **THORNTON** BSc in Special Maths. Was mathematics teacher in Leicester before joining in 1946, he left in 1952 to become senior maths master at King Edward IVth school, Kings Lynn.

A H **THURN.** After qualifying in Birmingham and Loughborough, and a post in Nuneaton, he joined Bemrose in 1939, leaving in 1950 when he moved to Buenos Aires. He reorganized the teaching of games and athletics. Honorary Coach to the Amateur Athletic Association.

TONKIN – a lady maths teacher described by John Brierley in his memoirs as "Blonde and steely eyed with a false smile". He found her intimidating, although her admired her trim bottom.

John Leslie **TRIPPETT,** taught French with a Yorkshire accent, possibly from Sheffield University where he gained his B.A and M.A degrees. Taught in Hertfordshire. He was also a qualified musician (LRAM) and taught Spanish from 1943 to 1959. Nicknamed "Rubber Gob".

Will **TUNNICLIFFE** was Maths teacher from 1938 to 1944 when he left for military service in the navy. His wife took his place on the staff until they left for Newcastle upon Tyne in 1946. He also taught at Brighton Road Secondary School, Derby.

Basil Stuart **TURNER** taught French, English and Divinity from 1932. Moved to Camelford, Cornwall. Died 1950. **M**

John Arthur **UNDERWOOD,** chemistry and biology teacher from 1964 to 1971 when he moved to Shelton Secondary School.

Malcolm Alastair **WARWICK** came from Wandsworth in 1958 to teach Russian and left in 1965 to become Head of Modern Languages at Scunthorpe Grammar school.

E Charles "Ikey" **WATTS,** art teacher at Bemrose for 35 years from 1921 to 1956. Died 1958. **M**

E H **WELLS** was Head of English from 1964-67.

S J "Stu" **WHEATLEY** taught science.

Fanny **WHETSTONE** taught biology. Married Ronnie Hanlon.

James Henry "Ben" **WILLETTS,** taught classics from 1967-1971 when he moved to Kilsyth Academy in Stirlingshire. He was involved in archaeology, but when Greek was phased out of the syllabus he was not replaced.

D **WILLIAMSON** 1962-67

Leslie Robert **WOOD,** joined the staff in 1930 to teach economics and geography, but left in 1938 to become assistant master at Bedales School.

Alan **WOODS,** married the school secretary Margaret Whetstone in 1951. He taught geography and moved on to become Head of geography at Manchester Grammar School. When he retired in 1983 he was Headmaster of Alleyne's Grammar School, Stone.

A **WORTLEY** taught classics from 1958-63.

R **WYCHERLEY** 1970-72

SCHOOL CAPTAINS From 1904-1986.

SCHOOL CAPTAINS.

1904 - 05.	A.M.THOMPSON.
1905 - 06.	C.A.SPENCER.
1906 - 07.	
1907 - 08.	H.BEAUMONT.
1908 - 09.	H.BEAUMONT.
1909 - 10.	W.HOWE.
1910 - 11.	S.L.LANCASTER.
1911 - 12.	R.G.ASHBY.
1912 - 13.	J.H.HARGREAVES.
1913 - 14.	W.E.BUSH.
1914 - 15.	G.A.PHILLIPS.
1915 - 16.	C.OTTEWELL.
1916 - 17.	E.A.TIMMS.
1917 - 18.	W.SHIRLEY.
1918 - 19.	R.C.L.EVELEIGH.
1919 - 20.	A.D.HILL.
1920 - 21.	A.FARQUHAR.
1921 - 22.	F.H.BIRKS.
1922 - 23.	O.TUNNICLIFF.
1923 - 24.	B.S.SOLOMON.
1924 - 25.	J.G.DUNNING.
1925 - 26.	C.LOVATT.
1926 - 27.	K.G.ROOK.
1927 - 28.	E.B.THOMSON.
1928 - 29.	J.M.BIRKS.
1929 - 30.	D.W.LOCKE.
1930 - 31.	D.W.LOCKE.
1931 - 32.	R.W.PATTINSON.
1932 - 33.	D.W.LANGFORD.
1933 - 34.	E.M.MAUNDER.
1934 - 35.	F.L.DRURY.
1935 - 36.	T.D.EATON.
1936 - 37.	P.J.HAYWOOD.
1937 - 38.	G.E.EMERY.
1938 - 39.	S.C.BREALEY.
1939 - 40.	A.H.H.YEOMANS.
1940 - 41.	W.N.ANDERSON.
1941 - 42.	A.G.C.WILLIAMS.
1942 - 43.	R.C.SOUTHERTON
1943 - 44.	D.J.COX.
1944 - 45.	R.J.D.PIMLEY.
1945 - 46.	K.COE.
1946 - 47.	L.ASHTON.
1947 - 48.	N.LONGDON.
1948 - 49.	K.HACKETT.
1949 - 50.	P.COLSTON.
1950 - 51.	J.F.RAYNES.
1951 - 52.	J.B.HEATH.
1952 - 53.	B.THOMPSON.
1953 - 54.	R.W.J.HUBANK.
1954 - 55.	J.E.HOWARTH.

SCHOOL CAPTAINS.

1955 - 56.	J.A.STANLEY.
1956 - 57.	M.J.ALLEN.
1957 - 58.	R.D.WILSON.
1958 - 59.	R.D.WILSON.
1959 - 60	H.ROSE.
1960 - 61.	R.D.A.JONES.
1961 - 62.	C.B.HATCH
1962 - 63.	P.D.SHARROCK
	D.A.KEELING
1963 - 64.	B.E.MOULDS
1964 - 65.	C.C.BUTLER
1965 - 66.	O.MAURER
1966 - 67.	J.N.LOUGHHEAD
1967 - 68.	K.A.SUDBURY
1968 - 69.	A.V.WOZNIAK
1969 - 70.	P.E.FRENCH
1970 - 71.	C.P.REDFERN
1971 - 72.	M.J.WASS
	D.M.KEETLEY
1972 - 73.	C.I.MACKENZIE
	M.P.B.BENNY
1973 - 74.	P.ROBINSON
1974 - 75.	P.A.JARRALD
1974 - 75.	R.B.DIXON
1975 - 76.	G.A.DAVISON
1975 - 76.	M.R.TURNER
1976 - 77.	J.S.ELLIOTT
1977 - 78.	A.J.W.WELLS
1978 - 79.	M.GRESHAM
1979 - 80.	C.A.BAXTER
1980 - 81.	P.WARRINGTON
1981 - 82	A.DAMJANOVIC
1982 - 83	L.COSBY
1983 - 84	M.ZINKUS
	M.BRIGGS
1984 - 85	C.KNIBBS
1985 - 86	K.SMITH

1904-05	A M THOMPSON	1947-48	N LONGDON
1905-06	C A SPENCER	1948-49	K HACKETT
1906-07		1949-50	P COLSTON
1907-08	H BEAUMONT	1950-51	J F RAYNES
1908-09	H BEAUMONT	1951-52	J B HEATH
1909-10	W HOWE	1952-53	B THOMPSON
1910-11	S L LANCASTER	1953-54	R W J HUBANK
1911-12	R G ASHBY	1954-55	J E HOWARTH
1912-13	I H HARGREAVES	1955-56	J A STANLEY
1913-14	W E BUSH	1956-57	M J ALLEN
1914-15	G A PHILLIPS	1957-59	R D WILSON
1915-16	C OTTEWELL	1959-60	H ROSE
1916-17	E A TIMMS	1960-61	R D A JONES
1917-18	W SHIRLEY	1961-62	C B HATCH
1918-19	R C L EVELEIGH	1962-63	P D SHARROCK, D A KEELING
1919-20	A D HILL		
1920-21	A FARQUHAR	1963-64	B E MOULDS
1921-22	F H BIRKS	1964-65	C C BUTLER
1922-23	O TUNNICLIFFE	1965-66	O MAURER
1923-24	B S SOLOMON	1966-67	J N LOUGHHEAD
1924-25	J G DUNNING	1967-68	K A SUDBURY
1925-26	C LOVATT	1968-69	A V WOZNIAK
1926-27	K G ROOK	1969-70	P E FRENCH
1927-28	E B THOMSON	1970-71	C P REDFERN
1928-29	J M BIRKS	1971-72	M J WASS, D M KEETLEY
1929-30	D W LOCKE		
1930-31	D W LOCKE	1972-73	C I MACKENZIE, M P B BENNY
1931-32	R W PATTINSON		
1932-33	D W LANGFORD	1973-74	P ROBINSON
1933-34	E M MAUNDER	1974-75	P A JARRALD, R B DIXON
1934-35	F L DRURY		
1935-36	T D EATON	1975-76	G A DAVIDSON, M R TURNER
1936-37	P J HAYWOOD		
1937-38	G E EMERY	1976-77	J S ELLIOTT
1938-39	S C BREARLEY	1977-78	A J W WELLS
1939-40	A H H YEOMANS	1978-79	M GRESHAM
1940-41	W N ANDERSON	1979-80	C A BAXTER
1941-42	A G C WILLIAMS	1980-81	P WARRINGTON
1942-43	R C SOUTHERTON	1981-82	A DAMIAMOVIC
1943-44	D J COX	1982-83	L COSBY
1944-45	R J D PIMLEY	1983-84	M ZINKUS, M BRIGGS
1945-46	K COE		
1946-47	L ASHTON	1984-85	C KNIBBS
		1985-86	K SMITH

THE WAR DEAD (Edited by Anton Rippon)

Lux Perpetua Luceat Eis (Their Light Forever Shines)

The following details are taken from the Bemrose School Book of Remembrance, and supplemented with details from the Commonwealth War Graves Commission. In two instances (marked thus★) no record has been found in the CWGC records available. Roger Hall and Robert George Hallam appear on the list of the School's fallen although no details of their years at Bemrose are available.

BANKS, John Rothwell (b.1917; School 1932-35) Lieut, 43rd Reconnaissance Corps, RAC. Killed in action in Normandy, 5 August 1944. Buried at Bayeux War Cemetery, France.

BENNETT, Hector Ernest (b.1918; School 1928-35) Sgt (Pilot), RAFVR. Killed 4 February 1941, crashed when making a forced landing in Wiltshire. Cremated at Bristol Crematorium.

BIRD, Joseph Ronald (b.1920; School 1931-36) Flt-Sgt, 218 Sqdn, RAFVR. Missing presumed killed on his 58th bombing operation, 27 August 1942. Commemorated on the Runnymede Memorial.

BOOTH, Geoffrey (b.1918; School 1926-33) Flying Officer, 103 Sqdn, RAF. Killed over Berlin, 26 November 1943. Buried at Berlin War Cemetery.

BOWERS, Frank (b.1924; School 1935-40) Sgt (Navigator), RAFVR. Killed 26 July 1944 in a bomber plane crash, taking off for night operations. Buried at St Peter's Churchyard, Littleover.

BRIERS, John Keith (b.1920; School 1932-37) Cadet LAC. Fatally injured at Cockram, Georgia, USA, while undergoing pilot training, 26 December 1941. Buried at Montgomery (Oakwood) Cemetery, Alabama, USA.

BROWN, Henry Shaw (b.1921; School 1931-37) Flt-Sgt, 174 Sqdn, RAF. Reported missing from operations, later presumed dead, 18 February 1944. Commemorated on the Runnymede Memorial.

BROWN, Logie Watson (b.1920; School 1928-37) Pilot Officer, 500 Sqdn, RAF. Posted missing on operation off Friesian Islands, 25 October 1941, later presumed killed. Commemorated on the Runnymede Memorial.

BULLIVANT, Douglas James (b.1920; School 1932-35) Able Seaman, Royal Navy, HMS Chasseur 06. Reported missing, 12 October 1940, later presumed killed. Commemorated on the Portsmouth Naval memorial.

BURGESS, Frederic Ralph Percival (b.1920; School 1931-34) Sgt (Pilot), RAFVR. Killed on active service, 21 March 1941. Buried at St Peter's Churchyard, Alstonfield.

BUXTON, William (b.1911; School 1922-27) Coder, HMS Wafney. Killed in action, 8 November 1942 (on the first ship to enter Oran, French North Africa). Commemorated on the Chatham Naval Memorial.

CLARKE, Archibald Frank Grafton (b.1897; School 1907-08) Major, Royal Indian Army Ordnance Corps. Died on service, 19 October 1941. Buried at Karachi War Cemetery, Pakistan.

COOK, Cyril Douglas (b.1918; School 1930-33) LAC, RAFVR. Killed by enemy action, Tripoli, 7 March 1943. Buried at Tripoli War Cemetery, Libya.

DAVIS, Maurice Henry (b.1920; School 1930-36) Trooper, RAC (9th Bn The Lancashire Fusiliers). Drowned in River Trent while taking part in military exercise, 27 June 1943. Buried at Ockbrook (Borrowash) Cemetery.

DELANY, John Raymond (b.1916; School 1929-35) Signalman, RCS. Killed on duty as a despatch rider, 23 September 1939. Buried at Uttoxeter Road Cemetery, Derby.

DOBSON, Albert (b.1920; School 1930-36) Sgt (Pilot), 148 Sqdn, RAFVR. Killed whilst returning to base after a night bombing raid over Syria, 7 July 1941. Buried at Fayid War Cemetery, Egypt.

DOVE, William (b.1921; School 1932-37) Sgt (Pilot), 424 Sqdn, RCAF. Killed in crash landing, 2 May 1943. Buried at Melbourne Cemetery, Derbyshire.

DOWDY, Eric Norman (b.1922; School 1933-38) Trooper, RAC ('D' Sqdn, 2nd Lothian and Borders Horse). Killed in action in Tunisia, 11 April 1943. Buried at Enfidaville War Cemetery, Tunisia.

DRAPER, Cecil (b.1919; School 1930-35) Trooper, 2nd Battalion, Royal Tank Regiment, RAC. Killed in action in the Middle East, 21 November 1941. Commemorated on the Alamein Memorial, Egypt.

DUNN, Harold Edward (b.1924; School 1935-41) Sub-Lieut, HMS Mergauser, RNVR. Killed in a flying accident at Cromarty, Scotland, 28 June 1945. Buried at Nottingham Road Cemetery, Derby.

EALES, William Norman (b.1915; School 1927-33) Flt-Lieut, 97 Sqdn, RAFVR (Rhodesian Air Force). Killed on bombing raid on Duisburg, 20 December 1943. Buried at Grosbeek Canadian War Cemetery, Holland.

EASTWOOD, William Benjamin (b.1916; School 1927-32) Sgt (Pilot), 10 Sqdn, RAFVR. Killed in action, 30 March 1942. Commemorated on the Runnymede Memorial.

ELLIOTT, Frank (b.1920; School 1931-36) Sgt, RAFVR. Killed in action, 15 July 1941. Commemorated on Runnymede Memorial.

ELWELL, Ernest Gordon (b.1922; School 1935-39) Sub-Lieut, HMS Indomitable (Fleet Air Arm), RNVR. Killed in flying accident, 19 November 1943. Buried at Nottingham Road Cemetery, Derby.

EVANS, Stanley (b.1912. School 1924-28) Flt-Lieut (Pilot), 7 Sqdn, RAFVR. Killed serving with Pathfinder Force in operations over Nuremberg, 31 March, 1944. Buried at Durnbach War Cemetery, Germany.

FEARY, Alan Norman (b.1912. School 1923-29) Flt-Sgt, 609 Sqdn, RAFVR. Shot down 7 October 1940. Buried at Holy Trinity Churchyard, Warmwell, Dorset. (Accounted for nine enemy planes around south coast of Britain. "His astonishing success in the air proved him to be one of our foremost and determined fighter pilots." Squadron Leader commanding 609 Sqdn.)

FREARSON, Ronald (b.1918; School 1930-34) Engine Room Artificer 4th Class, HMS Egret, RN. Died on service, 14 July 1944. Cremated at Nottingham.

GARNER, Edward (b.1921; School 1932-35) Sgt (Navigator), 35 Sqdn, RAF. Killed serving with Pathfinder Force in operations over Dusseldorf, 26 May 1943. Buried at Reichswald Forest War Cemetery, Germany.

GAUKROGER, Kenneth (b.1920; School 1934) Sgt (Rear Gunner), 37 Sqdn, RAF. Died in the Middle East, 21 October 1941. Buried at Suez War Memorial Cemetery, Egypt.

GEE, George Muir (b.1915; School 1926-31) Sgt (Pilot) RAFVR. Killed in crash landing, 14 January 1942. Buried at St Edmund's Churchyard, Allestree.

GEE, Ronald (b.1921; School 1932-38) Flying Officer (Navigator), RAF. Killed when his aircraft crashed into the sea, 6 March1944. Commemorated on the Runnymede Memorial.

GLEW, Norman (b.1916; School 1928-33) Sqdn Leader, 1435 Sqdn, RAFVR. Killed in action in Brindisi, Italy, 8 May 1944. Buried at Bari War Cemetery, Italy.

GRANGER, Harold Patrick (b.1920; School 1929-35) AC1, RAF. Died in captivity, 22 June 1945. Commemorated on the Singapore Memorial, Kranji War Cemetery, Singapore.

HALL, Roger Julius AC2, RAF. Died in captivity, 8 July 1943. Buried in Kanchanaburi War Cemetery, Thailand.

HALLAM, Robert Gerald (b.1920. *Editor's note: possibly in the Prep 1929*) 2nd Lieut, 25th Field Regt, RA. Died 13 December 1941. Commemorated on the Alamein Memorial, Egypt.

HARRIS, John Frederick (b.1923; School 1935-39) AC2, RAFVR. Killed in Southern Rhodesia, 28 August 1943. Buried at Athlone Cemetery, Bulawayo, Zimbabwe.

HOLMES, Edward (b.1920; School 1931-36) Lance Corporal, RAMC (attached to 59 Light AA Regiment, RA). Killed by enemy action during an air-raid on Sheffield, 12-13 December 1940. Buried at St Peter's Churchyard, Littleover.

HOWELL, Kenneth Brian (b.1923; School 1933-38) Flt-Sgt, 186 Sqdn, RAFVR. Missing, presumed killed, on operations over Duisberg, Germany, 14 October 1944. Commemorated on the Runnymede Memorial.

IRONMONGER, Ernest James (b.1921; School 1932-38) Flt-Sgt (Wireless Operator/Air Gunner), 78 Sqdn, RAFVR. Killed while on operational flight to Germany, 10 August 1942. Buried at Bergen-op-Zoom War Cemetery, Holland.

JOHNSON, Sydney Wallace (b.1920; School 1935-36) Sgt (Wireless Operator /Air Gunner), 40 Sqdn, RAFVR. Killed in France, 14 June 1940. Buried at Garancieres-en-Drouais Communal Cemetery, France.

LANGLEY, John Eli (b.1923; School 1936-39) Telegraphist, HMS Avonvale. Missing on operations in the Mediterranean, later presumed killed, 29 January 1943. Commemorated on the Plymouth Naval Memorial.

LEE, Maurice Gordon (b.1928; School 1939-43) Private, 2nd Btn, Sherwood Foresters. Killed in Jewish terrorist outrage in Palestine, 1 March 1947. Buried at Khayat War Cemetery, Israel.

LEES, Peter Henry George (b.1923; School 1933-39) Sgt (Bomb Aimer), 31 Sqdn, RAFVR. Killed on operations, 14 August 1944. Buried at Krakow Rakowicki Cemetery, Poland.

LESTER, Gordon (b.1925; School 1936-41) Sgt (Air Gunner) 576 Sqdn, RAFVR. Killed over Luxemburg after raid on Wiesbaden, Germany, 3 February 1945. Buried at Hotton War Cemetery, Belgium.

LEWSLEY, Alfred James (b.1920; School 1930-36) Flt-Lieut (Navigator), 78 Sqdn, RAFVR. Killed on operations over Harborg, Germany, 4 April 1945. Buried at Becklingen War Cemetery, Germany.

⋆McCLEMONT, Patrick Douglas (b.1923; School 1932-40) Flt-Sgt, 166 Sqdn, RAF. Killed on a night flying bomber operation from RAF Kirmington, Lincolnshire, 8 October 1945.

McKIM, Eric (b.1921; School 1930-35) Sgt, 210 Sqdn, RAFVR. Missing, presumed killed, while on operations over the Bay of Biscay, 22 March 1943. Commemorated on the Malta Memorial.

MASON, Eric (b.1910; School 1921-27) Sgt (Wireless Operator /Air Gunner), 214 Sqdn, RAFVR. Killed over Belgium on first operational flight, 13 April 1942. Buried at Heverlee War Cemetery, Belgium.

MATTHEWS, Francis Norman (b.1912; School 1923-29) Corporal, 241 Sqdn, RAFVR. Killed in enemy raid on his airfield in Italy, 30 September 1944. Buried at Coriano Ridge War Cemetery, Italy.

MOCKRIDGE, Frederick (b.1918; School 1930-35) Flt-Sgt, 58 Sqdn, RAFVR. Killed in action, 16 October 1940. Commemorated on the Runnymede Memorial.

MOORLEY, Maurice Rupert (b.1913; School 1925-29) Flying Officer (Pilot Instructor), RAFVR. Killed on service, 10 September 1942. Buried at All Saints' Churchyard, Mickleover.

MOSELEY, Leonard Granville (b.1920; School 1930-35) Flt-Sgt, 51 Sqdn, RAFVR. Killed on service, 6 February 1943. Buried at All Saints' Churchyard, Mickleover.

MUDD, Arthur Gordon (Jim) (b.1924; School 1937-40) Sgt (Pilot), RAFVR. Killed while piloting a Wellington bomber over Egypt, 21 March 1944. Buried at El Alamein war Cemetery, Egypt.

MURPHY, John Joseph (b.1924; School 1935-40) Sgt (Flight Engineer), 433 (RCAF) Sqdn, RAFVR. Killed over Leipzig, 20 February 1944. Buried at Berlin 1939-45 War Cemetery.

PAGE, John Reginald (b.1921; School 1934-37) Flt-Sgt (Navigator/Bomb-aimer), RAFVR. Killed in flying accident over Norway, 4 January 1946. Buried at Eiganes Churchyard, Stavanger, Norway.

PARKER, William (b.1918; School 1929-34) LAC, RAFVR. Killed at Monastir, Tunisia, 28 April 1943. Buried at Enfidaville War Cemetery, Tunisia.

PETERS, Francis (b.1921; School 1933-37) AC2, RAFVR. Killed between Burton and Lichfield while on service, 14 September 1944. Buried at Normanton Cemetery, Derby.

POYSER, Donald Arthur (b.1921; School 1932-36) Sgt (Wireless Operator/Air Gunner), RAFVR. Died 1 March 1941. Buried at Nottingham Road Cemetery, Derby.

POXON, William Hollingworth (b.1922; School 1933-37) Coder, HMS Prince of Wales, RN. Lost when HMS Prince of Wales was sunk by Japanese forces off Malaya, 10 December 1941. Commemorated at Plymouth Naval Memorial.

RAWCLIFFE, Richard (b.1921; School 1931-36) Sgt (Observer), RAFVR. Missing from anti-submarine operations 17 December 1942, later presumed dead. Commemorated on the Runnymede Memorial.

REEVES, George Verney (b.1915; School 1928-32) Sgt (Observer), 206 Sqdn, RAFVR. Killed while returning from operations, 21 April 1941. Buried at Nottingham Road Cemetery, Derby.

RENSHAW, Charles William (b.1919; School 1928-33) Trooper, 2nd Fife and Forfar Yeomanry, RAC. Killed in action, North-West Europe, 18 July 1944. Commemorated on the Bayeux Memorial.

RUDGE, Maurice Henry (b.1918; School 1929-35) Sub Conductor (WO1), RAOC. Died on active service, 29 July 1946. Buried at St Peter's Churchyard, Littleover, Derby.

SAMUEL, Donald John (b.1907; School 1918-22) Ordinary Seaman, HMS Picotee, RN. Killed when HMS Picotee was lost with all hands south of Iceland, 12 August 1941. Commemorated on the Chatham Naval Memorial.

SMART, Trevor Tressler, DFC (b.1923; School 1934-40) Flying Officer, 207 Sqdn, RAFVR. Missing on operation near Cologne, 22 June 1944, later presumed killed. Commemorated on the Runnymede Memorial. (Immediate award of DFC, 19-20 May 1944. "Flying Officer Smart, who has only four sorties to his credit, showed great courage, determination and exceptional airmanship in successfully bringing the aircraft back home")

SMITH, Francis Melville (b.1908; School 1919-25) Flying Officer (Air Bomber), 12 Sqdn, RAFVR. Killed when his Lancaster bomber exploded over the Firth of Forth, 7 July 1943. Buried at St Michael's Churchyard, Alvaston.

SOAR, William Godfrey (b.1913; School 1925-29) Lieutenant, 3 HAA Regt, RA. Died in captivity, 11 November 1943. Buried in Kanchanaburi War Cemetery, Thailand.

STAPLEFORD, Wilfred Holmes (b.1915; School 1926-34) Captain, RAMC. Died in Berlin, 13 October 1945. Buried at Berlin 1939-45 War Cemetery.

STEVENSON, Alexander Bertram (b.1920; School 1929-35) Sgt (Air Gunner), RAFVR. Missing over the Irish Sea, 22 May 1943, later presumed killed. Commemorated on the Runnymede Memorial.

TOOTH, John Ernest (b.1923; School 1934-39; Derby Cathedral chorister) Flt-Sgt (Air Bomber), 625 Sqdn, RAF. Killed 13 September 1944. Buried at Durnbach War Cemetery, Germany.

TOPHAM, Leonard Webster (b.1909; School 1920-25) AC2, RAFVR. Died on service, 13 September 1942. Cremated at Nottingham Crematorium.

TROTT, James Henry (b.1918; School 1929-34) Captain, 65th Field Regt, RA. Died of wounds in Italy, 12 September 1944. Buried at Ancona War Cemetery, Italy.

TURNER, Kenneth (b.1921; School 1931-38) LAC, RAF. Lost at sea after his troopship was torpedoed en route to South Africa, 5 July 1941. Commemorated on the Runnymede Memorial.

*VAN SCHAICK, John Edward, DFC (b.1921; School 1932-37) Flt-Lieut, RAF. Killed on active service, 20 February 1943. (Awarded DFC, November 1941. "This airman has participated in 200 operational sorties and has proved to be a keen and reliable pilot who has destroyed several hostile aircraft").

WALKER-SMITH, Francis Richard (b.1917; School 1929-34) Pilot Officer, 85 Sqdn, RAFVR. Killed while flying as a passenger in an American Havoc plane from RAF Debden, Essex, 13 March 1941. Buried at Saffron-Walden Cemetery, Essex. (Mentioned in Despatches, 1941)

WALLACE, Alec Henry (b.1906; School 1916-23) Trooper, 18th (5th Btn, The Loyal Regt) Regt, Reconnaissance Corps. Died from cholera while in captivity working on the Burma Railway, 4 June 1943. Buried at Thanbyuzayat War Cemetery, Myanmar.

WALTERS, Edwin Whysall (b.1916; School 1927-34) Flt-Sgt (Observer), 22 Sqdn, RAF. Killed on operation over France, 2 December 1941. Buried at Pont-du-Cens Communal Cemetery, Nantes, France.

WALTON, Raymond Thomas (b.1924; School 1934-40) Private, Northamptonshire Regt. Killed in action at the Battle of Anzio, 1 May 1944. Buried at Anzio Beachhead War Cemetery, Italy.

WARDEL KNIGHT, Eric Cecil (b.1920; School 1928-35) Sgt (Pilot), 142 Sqdn, RAFVR. Killed 20 September 1940. Buried at St Peter's Churchyard, Littleover.

WARREN, Albert George (b.1916; School 1926-35) Flt-Lieut (Navigator), 53 Sqdn, RAFVR. Failed to return from escort patrol over the Atlantic, 21 November 1943; presumed killed. Commemorated on the Runnymede Memorial.

WATSON, George William Lewis (b.1920; School 1932-36) Third Radio Officer, SS Muneric, Merchant Navy. Killed when his ship was torpedoed off Cape Farewell, Greenland, 10 September 1941. Commemorated on the Tower Hill Memorial.

WRIGHT, Kenneth William (b.1921; School 1934-39) Sgt (Pilot), RAFVR. Killed on active service, 25 February 1943. Buried at St Peter's Churchyard, Littleover.

WRIGHT Ronald Alfred (b.1923; School 1934-39) Sgt (Pilot), RAFVR. Killed on active service, 28 September 1944. Buried at St Peter's Churchyard, Littleover.

YARKER, Thomas (b.1923; School 1934-39) Sgt (Navigator/Wireless Operator), 84 Sqdn, RAFVR. Killed in flying accident in India, 5 March 1945. Buried at Madras War Cemetery, Chennai, India.

School War Memorial Dedicated

A wall panel in Bemrose School, Derby, library, bearing the names of former pupils who lost their lives in the 1939-45 war, was unveiled and dedicated by the Archdeacon of Derby the Venerable H. E. Fitz-Herbert).

Mr. N. A. Taylor, vice-president of the Old Bemrosians' Association, handed to the Headmaster (Mr. W. A. Macfarlane) a commemorative book, bound in red calf skin with gilt lettering, to be kept in the school library.

Subscribed for by Old Bemrosians, the book contains photographs and personal details of each man. It is hoped to add citations later.

Nearly 300 people attended the service, including parents and relatives of the fallen men.

The Deputy Mayor (Councillor G. F. Warburton) and the Director of Education for Derby (Mr. C. Middleton) were among those present.